DIESEL TROUBLESHOOTER

DIESEL TROUBLESHOOTER

Don Seddon

fernhurst
BOOKS

First published 1996 by Fernhurst Books, Duke's Path, High Street,
Arundel, West Sussex, BN18 9AJ, UK

Printed and bound in Great Britain

British Library Cataloguing in Publication Data:
A catalogue record for this book is available from the British Library.

ISBN 1 898660 21 2

Acknowledgments
The author and publisher would like to thank Motor Boat & Yachting
magazine for use of some of the diagrams and Lister Marine Diesels for
their help with the photo sessions, and the following organisations for
information and support:
Lister Marine Diesels
Motor Boat and Yachting
Robert Bosch Ltd
E.P.Barrus Ltd
BP
Perkins Engines
Vetus UK
and numerous boat owning friends who have provided much useful
material for the troubleshooting sections.

Photographic credits
Cover photos courtesy of Lister Marine Diesels
All other photos by Chris Davies except Intrum Justitia (p2),
Perkins Marine Power Centre (p50), MB & Y (P71).

Edited by Adrian Morgan and Tom Willis
DTP by Creative Byte, Bournemouth
Cover design by Simon Balley
Printed by Hillman Printers, Frome
Text set in 10pt Rockwell Light

Contents

FOREWORD

At sea on tidal waters, or on rivers and inland waterways, a reliable diesel engine is essential. Rescue statistics confirm how many emergencies could have been avoided if the boat's most basic item of safety equipment, its diesel engine, had been properly maintained.

This book not only aims to give boat owners a basic understanding of how a diesel works – and what to do to keep it in good running order – but also to enable them to 'troubleshoot' any faults that may occur.

I hope you will find it a useful addition to your boat's library. Much of the subject is covered in diesel engine courses, so I hope boat owners who have attended one of these useful courses will also find it a good reference book and an *aide-memoire* to keep handy afterwards.

Don Seddon
January 1996

1 How it works

The diesel is the simplest of all engines, which is one of the main reasons for its reputation as the most reliable power source for ships and boats. Despite all the technological advances made by man, simplicity is still the key to reliability.

At its most basic, the diesel needs only fuel and air to operate. There is no electrical ignition system: the engine works on the principle that if you compress a gas its temperature rises. This, incidentally, gives the diesel its alternative name of compression ignition engine, to distinguish it from spark ignition (petrol) engines.

In a diesel, the fuel is injected into a cylinder containing superheated compressed air. The heat ignites the fuel-air mixture, which expands as it burns, and the resulting pressure drives a piston downwards. The piston is connected by a rod to a crankshaft, which converts the downward thrust of the piston into the

This gearbox-end view of a four-cylinder marine diesel shows the built-in brass oil-change pump (1) and screw-in oil filter (2) with starter solenoid immediately above it.

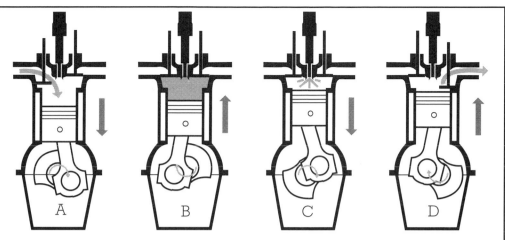

Four-stroke diesel cycle
A. Induction. Piston descends, inlet valve opens and air is drawn into the cylinder.
B. Compression. Piston rises. The air is compressed and heated to around 700°C. Near the top of the stroke a fine spray of diesel is injected into the cylinder.
C. Power. The air/diesel mixture is ignited by the hot air and the piston is driven down.
D. Exhaust. Exhaust valve opens and the spent gases are expelled.

rotary torque needed to drive the propeller.

There are some two-stroke diesel engines, but the majority operate on the four-stroke cycle. As its name implies, the full cycle consists of four strokes of the piston, two upward and two downward: induction, compression, power and exhaust. This gives one power stroke per two revolutions of the crankshaft.

The illustration above shows the full sequence, beginning with the induction stroke. As the piston descends the inlet valve opens and a charge of air is drawn into the cylinder. When the piston reaches the bottom of its stroke the valve closes.

The piston now starts travelling upwards on the compression stroke, pressurising the air trapped in the cylinder. By the time the piston reaches the top and all the air has been squeezed into the combustion chamber at the top of the cylinder, the temperature of the air will have risen to around 500-700°C.

At this point fuel is injected into the combustion chamber in the form of an atomised spray. The hot air and fuel mixture ignites in a controlled explosion, the pressure forcing the piston down again on its power stroke.

After the power stroke the piston rises on the exhaust stroke, propelled by the still-turning crankshaft. As it rises the exhaust valve opens and the burnt gases are expelled. At the top of the stroke the exhaust valve then closes and the cycle begins again.

The temperature generated in the

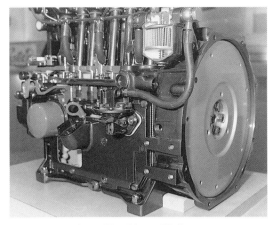

Above and right: The Lister Alpha range was designed specifically for small boats and will develop from 20-40hp. This cutaway example for exhibition use shows the rugged cylinder construction necessary to withstand the forces of compression. Note too the fine filter (top right, above) and the heavy flywheel to smooth output.

combustion chamber depends on how much the air is compressed – normally between 16:1 and 25:1 for diesel engines.. This figure, the compression ratio, is calculated by dividing the volume of the combustion chamber when the piston is at the top of its stroke into the volume of the much larger enclosed space when the piston reaches the bottom of its stroke.

All four-stroke engines need a weight in the form of a flywheel to carry the crankshaft smoothly through the three non-power strokes. When the engine first fires, the initial power stroke turns the crankshaft, after which the momentum of the flywheel keeps the crankshaft turning, driving the piston up and down, until the next power stroke.

A single-cylinder engine needs a large flywheel relative to its size. Because a

multi-cylinder engine staggers the piston power strokes there is less work for the flywheel, which can be correspondingly smaller and lighter. For added smoothness, crankshafts also incorporate balance weights and are statically and dynamically balanced to keep out-of-balance forces to a minimum.

In some cases secondary balance shafts are incorporated, driven from the crankshaft. These directly counterbalance the forces created by the power stroke, reduce engine vibration and thus enable a lighter flywheel to be used.

Geared to the crankshaft, and therefore rotating as it rotates, are the high pressure injection pump, the camshaft which controls the inlet and exhaust valves, the fuel lift pump, the water pumps and the alternator.

The quality and efficiency of combustion, and therefore the power developed, is determined by the quantity of fuel injected (controlled by the throttle setting), the

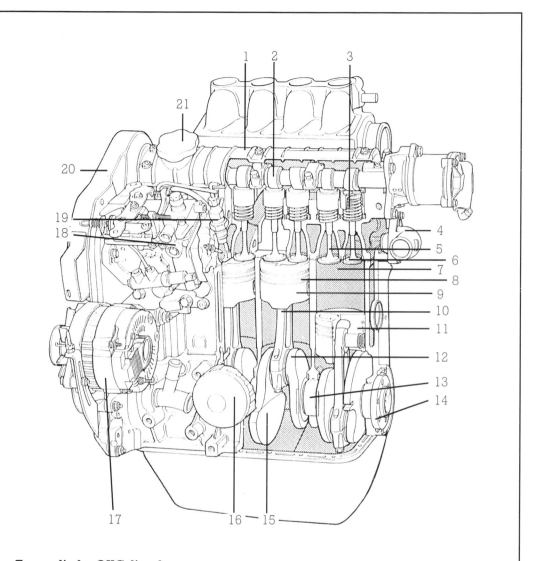

Four-cylinder OHC diesel

*1 Rocker cover. 2 Camshaft. 3 Valve spring. 4 Cooling water inlet. 5 Inlet valve.
6 Exhaust valve. 7 Cylinder. 8 Piston rings. 9 Piston. 10 Connecting rod. 11 Gudgeon pin.
12 Crank. 13 Main bearing. 14 Flywheel coupling. 15 Balance weight. 16 Oil filter.
17 Alternator. 18 Fuel injection pump. 19 Injector. 20 Camshaft drive gear. 21 Oil filler.*

diameter (bore) of the cylinder and the distance travelled by the piston (stroke), and the design of the combustion chamber. The actual output torque (turning force) at the crankshaft will also depend on the engine load, ie how much it is being required to work.

2 Fuel

Diesel fuel systems consist of two parts, a low pressure system and a high pressure system, and a number of different elements, all vital to the smooth running of the engine. The function of the low pressure side is to deliver a clean supply of uncontaminated fuel to the injection pump, but on the high pressure side it is just as important to ensure that the system remains free of debris and water contamination. The various elements are, in order:

Low pressure system
1. Fuel tank.
2. Supply line (with shut-off valve).
3. Pre-filter (water separating filter).
4. Fuel lift pump.
5. Engine fine filter.

High pressure system
6. Injection pump.

7. Injectors. Both the pump and the injectors process more fuel than is actually used. Excess fuel (leak off) is returned to the fine filter or the tank.

Fuel tank
This should ideally be above the engine level where the head of fuel will provide a positive pressure throughout the fuel system. Any leaks will then result in fuel seeping out rather than air being drawn in. If the tank is alongside or lower than the engine, and a leak develops, air can be drawn into the system when the engine is stopped. A small header tank will provide a positive pressure, but must be vented to the outside to allow flow into the engine fuel system.

Tanks can be made of various materials:
1. Stainless steel – of welded construction,

Modern fine fuel filters, like this Lucas one, are disposable. To change, simply unscrew the old filter using a strap if necessary. Fit the new one, which needs to be tightened only to hand pressure. A smear of fuel on the sealing ring will help it seat properly. The fuel line will then need to be bled to remove air from the system.

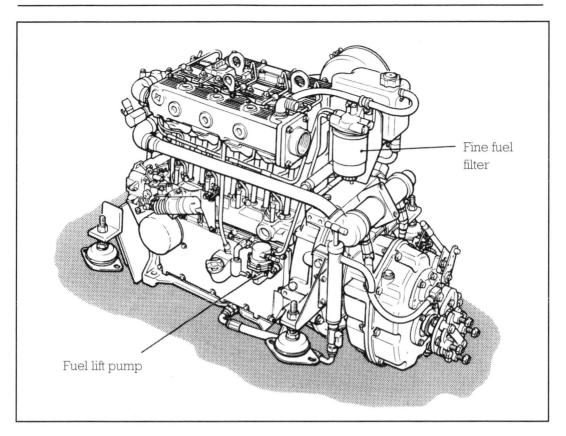

Fine fuel
filter

Fuel lift pump

strong and corrosion resistant.

2. Mild steel – of welded construction,
coated inside and out with a suitable
paint system, to protect against
corrosion.

3. Plastic – normally manufactured
from polythene and translucent so that
the fuel level can be seen. There is less
risk of condensation and no risk of rust
forming.

4. Heavy-duty flexible tanks – ideal as
temporary tanks for a long voyage or
for use in irregular spaces.

Supply line

Engines vibrate relative to the boat, and
therefore a fuel system made entirely of
solid pipe would soon fracture. Part of the
pipework between the tank and the engine

must be flexible, purpose-made hose with
a protective wire mesh cover. This is
normally fitted next to the engine, between
the water separator and the lift pump and in
the return from the system to the tank,
allowing the rest of the fuel line to be made
of solid pipe and securely fastened to the
boat.

The solid piping can be made of thick-
walled copper, bundy or stainless steel.
End fittings are either brazed-on ferrules or
swaged – olive-type fittings should not be
used. All sealing joints should be metal-to-
metal, and sealing compound or PTFE tape
must not be used because of the risk of
particles entering the fuel system.

The fuel isolator or fuel shut-off valve must

The engine's first line of defence is the pre-filter (water separator), fitted down line from the tank. Periodically drain off any water collected via the bottom drain screw and let the flow run until pure fuel emerges. Retighten the screw.

Water, the diesel's main enemy, is heavier than fuel. This was drained from a pre-filter on a yacht in mid-season. Even small amounts will stop an engine.

be as close to the fuel tank as possible, placed to allow someone to cut off the supply without entering the engine compartment in the event of a fire.

On the high pressure side, fittings using copper or aluminium face seals should be tightened just enough to start compressing the seal material. Be careful not to overtighten. The high pressure pipework between the high pressure pump and the injectors is carefully sized thick wall steel pipe. Both the length and the inside diameter are important relative to the dynamics of the system, to ensure that fuel delivered to the injectors is at the correct pressure. If the pipework needs to be

replaced, make sure you use genuine replacement parts from the engine manufacturer.

Fuel pre-filter or water trap

Water may pass through fine filters, so most systems have a separate water trap in which water can settle out of the fuel and be drained off periodically.

Fuel passes through the internal passages of a simple labyrinth which allows water and debris to settle out. This is then drained off by opening the small tap in the bottom. Catch and examine the liquid for signs of water or contamination. If there are more than a few drops of water, a jelly of water/oil or a small amount of debris,

Diesel fuel system

1. Pre-filter (water separator)
2. Drain cock
3. Fuel lift pump
4. Fine filter
5. Drain cock
6. In-line fuel injection pump
7. Mechanical governor housing
8. Speed control lever
9. Auto-advance coupling
10. Cold-start (extra fuel) button
11. Engine stop
12. Boost control unit
13. Delivery valve holder
14. Anti-stall device
15. High pressure fuel pipe
16. Atomiser (injector)

Typical venting (bleeding) points

A. Fine fuel filter
B. Injection pump
C. Injector

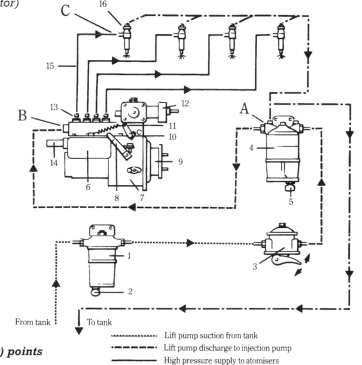

From tank To tank

.... Lift pump suction from tank
– – – – – – Lift pump discharge to injection pump
————— High pressure supply to atomisers
–·—·—·— Leak off back to tank

Above and right: This Vetus fuel tank has a fuel outlet pipe, fuel return pipe, vent pipe to open air and fuel level sensor wire. Baffles inside the tank help prevent the fuel surging as the vessel rolls, reducing the risk of the fuel becoming aerated or contaminated by sediment.

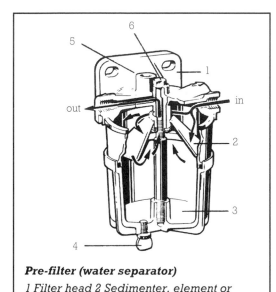

Pre-filter (water separator)
*1 Filter head 2 Sedimenter, element or
diffuser 3 Sedimenter chamber 4 Drain
plug 5 Venting point 6 Central fixing bolt*

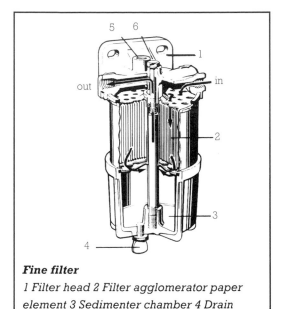

Fine filter
*1 Filter head 2 Filter agglomerator paper
element 3 Sedimenter chamber 4 Drain
plug 5 Venting point 6 Central bolt*

inspect the tank and if possible clean it out. The water trap does not need maintenance, but the cylindrical container can be taken out and cleaned if it is badly contaminated.

Most water separating filters consist of a disposable element filter, fitted above a clear plastic cup as a water trap, so that you can see if there is any water or dirt in the bottom. Give this a routine glance, and drain out any dirt/water if necessary. If this needs to be done often, then it indicates that the tank needs cleaning.

If the water trap is fitted with a filter element (as most are), you must change this at least as often as you change the fine filter. The pre-filter, as it is first in line, is more likely to clog than the fine filter.

Lift pump

This is operated continuously from a cam on the engine camshaft. It provides a

constant supply of fuel at low pressure to the high pressure injector pump, keeping it topped up. Some pumps have internal mesh screens to filter out debris in the fuel which could cause the non-return valves to stay open. This screen should be cleaned whenever a fine filter is changed.

The pump normally has an oscillating diaphragm, worked by a lever from the camshaft. Two non-return valves allow flow into and out of the chamber above the diaphragm. Once the pressure in the injector pump body is established the spring which returns the diaphragm becomes compressed and the displacement of the diaphragm becomes just enough to maintain the pressure.

A hand priming lever duplicates the function of the cam. If the lever won't move more than a little when you are priming or bleeding the system, turn the engine on the

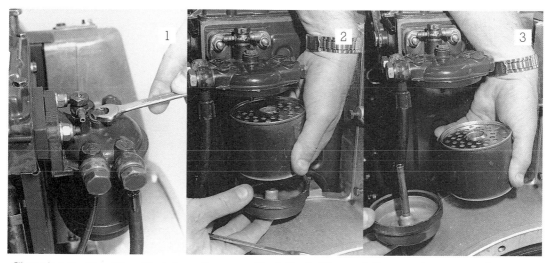

*Changing the fine filter. First clean the area of fuel. Drain filter and dispose of contents ashore
responsibly. 1 Unscrew central bolt. 2 Twist and pull base of filter to release. Discard old filter
element and replace, having cleaned filter bowl and sealing ring grooves with lint-free cloth.
3 Reassemble but don't overtighten bolt. Bleed fuel system.*

starter motor, or hand crank until the cam
allows more lever movement.

Lift pumps are not highly stressed and
rarely fail but you may want to carry spare
diaphragms and other parts, or even a
complete pump.

Fine fuel filter

The final line of defence for the high
pressure pump is the fine filter, which traps
any debris before it can clog either pump
or injectors.

The fine filter element – most often a
throwaway item, like an oil filter – should
be changed at the same time as the
lubricating oil filter. Take care to ensure
that the seals on the element or bowl, and
the holding bolts, are in good condition and
placed correctly. Only fit the
manufacturer's recommended replacement
filter, matched to the pump's requirements.

High pressure injection pump

Fuel is considered to be incompressible.
When it is pumped into a closed system the
pressure rises rapidly until the break
setting of the injector is reached, which for
non-turbo engines is normally
approximately 140 times atmospheric
pressure. The fuel then bursts through the
injector and out into the combustion
chamber in a fine atomised spray.

The pump timing has to be set so that
injection starts just before the piston
reaches the top of the compression stroke.

Diesel fuel is relatively thin, and the fit
between the hardened steel pump piston
and its housing has to be extremely close to
prevent fuel leaking out and consequent
loss of pressure. The pistons and valves
inside the pump which generate the
pressure are therefore manufactured using

Bleeding the fuel system

After changing the filter element, the
fuel system must be bled to remove
any air. First identify, then open the
bleed screw on the filter housing
(above right). Work the hand priming
lever on the lift pump until clear fuel
without bubbles flows out. Keep
pumping as the bleed screw is
tightened down (below right). This is
normally the high point in the low
pressure system. If it is not then it may
be necessary to bleed air from
another point, or even the high
pressure injector pump.

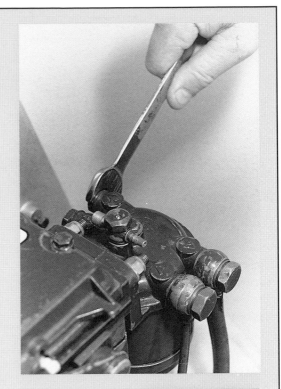

If the engine does need bleeding from
the high pressure injector pump, refer
to the manufacturer's instructions. It is
easy to undo the wrong screw on the
pump and upset the settings.

Many modern engines incorporate
self-bleeding devices which can cope
with minor leakages.

If a fuel-assisted cold starting device is
fitted, this too may need to be bled.
Undo one of the pipe union nuts and
follow the same procedure as the
bleed screw, and keep pumping as
the nut is tightened.

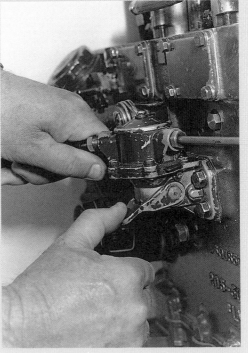

The injectors on this engine can clearly be seen. The prominent central pipes deliver fuel at high pressure from the pump while the smaller pipes drain the excess (leak-off) fuel back into the system.

hardened steel to very fine tolerances, with running clearances measured in thousandths of a millimetre (microns).

Sometimes individual pumps driven by a common camshaft supply individual injectors, or a single piston pump may supply several injectors by means of a distributor valve. In other cases several pumping elements are grouped together in a common housing.

In all cases the stroke of the piston, and therefore the amount of fuel delivered at pressure to the injector, is controlled mechanically. This controls the engine speed.

Most pumps incorporate a method of governing the engine by controlling the maximum fuel delivered. This provides constant speed regardless of load and also controls the maximum speed.

Slow speed setting (tickover) and fuel cut-off valves are also incorporated in this

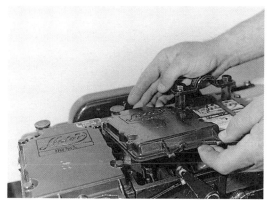

The injectors on this engine are sited under the rocker box cover, shown here being lifted off, and are clamped to the engine block.

complex and highly engineered part of the fuel system.

Servicing and tuning the pump should only be carried out by qualified personnel. The best the owner can do is keep the pipe fittings leak-free. He can also ensure that the bolts holding a rotary pump to the engine are kept tight. If not the timing can be changed as the pump moves within the clearance of the bolt holes. Finally he can lubricate the linkages.

Any pump that is driven by a timing belt should be inspected and the belt changed according to the manufacturer's instructions. Make sure that it does not slip otherwise incorrect timing will result in the engine failing to start, or running erratically.

Injector pumps rely on the diesel fuel passing through to lubricate them. Any water allowed into the pump will cause wear and possibly seizure of the parts.

Injectors

Injectors work like a relief valve. The internal piston is spring loaded, remaining

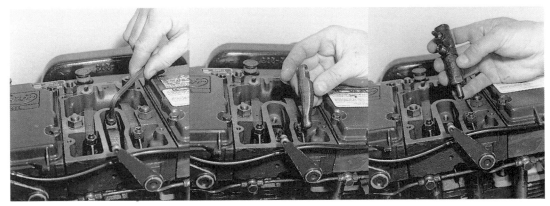

Once the rocker box cover has been unbolted, the clamp holding the injector is slackened, using an Allen key. The injector can then be lifted out. It is possible to check the spray pattern by reconnecting high pressure and leak-off pipes and turning the engine over, but be warned. Fuel is toxic and under high pressure can penetrate skin or damage eyes.

closed as pressure builds and opening when the set pressure (break setting) is reached. Fuel then squirts in very fine jets into the engine through several tiny holes in the end of the injector. The spring ensures that the opening and closing times are very precise. The precise amount of fuel required, as determined by the fuel pump speed control setting, will enter the combustion chamber. The injector itself does not control the amount of fuel. It just opens and allows through the amount being pumped into it.

Some injectors can be serviced, others are throwaway items. They can, however, last a considerable time – over 1,000 running hours if serviced properly. Always follow the maker's service recommendations.

Sticking injectors may make the engine difficult to start. They may be opening at a higher pressure than ideal and allowing less fuel into the combustion chamber. In this case they should either be serviced by a qualified engineer or exchanged for new ones or a complete service exchange set.

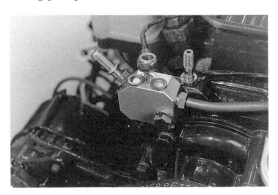

The pipes to and from this leak-off return rely on copper or aluminium washers for sealing. If there is a leak either fit new washers or clean the old ones. Copper, but not aluminium, washers should be annealed by heating until cherry red then allowed to cool. This softens them for better sealing.

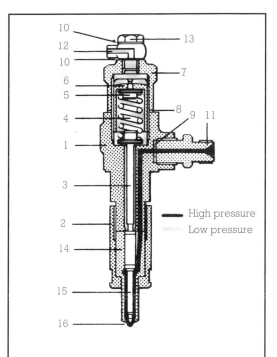

Multi-hole injector

*1 Nozzle holder. 2 Nozzle nut. 3 Spindle.
4 Spring. 5 Upper spring plate. 6 Spring
cap nut. 7 Cap nut. 8, 9, 10 Joint washers.
11 Inlet adaptor. 12 Leak-off connection.
13 Banjo bolt. 14 Nozzle. 15 Needle valve.
16 Spray holes.*

It is possible to take an injector out and then turn the engine over to check if fuel is being squirted through it. But we do not advise it. WARNING. Fuel jets, under enormous pressure, will easily penetrate the skin, or blind an eye. The fuel is also highly toxic.

The pockets in which the injectors sit are often sleeved, and the end of the injector is always sealed against the cylinder head to stop air and combustion gases leaking past. It is wise to remove the injectors, whether or not they need servicing, every few years to clean the sleeves, and ensure that they are not seized in by rust. Don't drop any debris into the engine, and refit with new sealing washers, if fitted.

Starting aids

Most diesel engines need a cold starting aid. In some cases extra fuel is injected directly into the combustion chamber, which has the effect of increasing the compression ratio. In other cases the injector pump has an override device which allows extra fuel through the injectors.

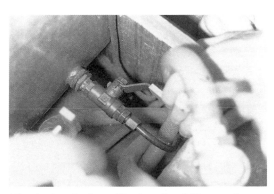

The fuel tank shut-off valve should be as close as possible to the tank, and outside the engine compartment in case it needs to be turned off in the event of a fire.

Decompression levers, or valve lifters, open the exhaust valves, enabling the engine to be turned more easily by hand. Once up to cranking speed the levers are dropped and the engine should then fire.

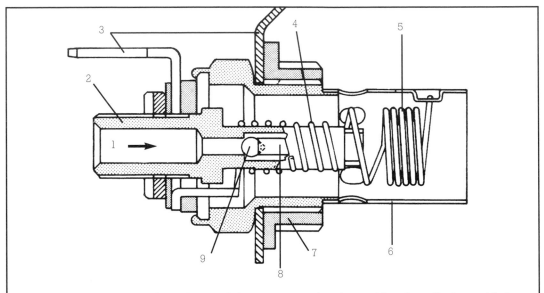

This Lucas Thermostart, fitted in the air intake, warms the air reaching the cylinder and helps the engine start in cold weather. A small quantity of diesel, released through a ball valve which is opened by a heater coil, is then burnt by an electric igniter coil. 1 Fuel inlet. 2 Body. 3 Electric terminals. 4 Heater coil. 5 Igniter coil. 6 Igniter shield. 7 Insulating bush. 8 Needle valve stem. 9 Ball valve.

Many engines have electric glow plugs in the combustion chamber area to heat and ignite the air fuel mixture. Others have electric inlet manifold heating elements which warm the air flowing in. This is sometimes combined with the introduction of fuel into the manifold. This burns in the manifold, warming the engine and helping it to start.

Occasionally, if the engine is fairly old, a small dose of quickstart squirted into the inlet manifold can help. Some manufacturers specifically ban this, as it can build up in the exhaust system and explode, destroying the exhaust when the engine starts.

Valve lifters (decompression levers) are fitted to many smaller engines, and are obligatory for a hand start. These open the exhaust valves, relieving compression. This enables the engine to build up speed and therefore momentum. The valves are then closed and the normal compression cycle begins.

An engine may start easily in summer without any cold start aid, but if it does not it is better to use the cold start procedure to ensure a quick start rather than risk draining the battery by repeated unsuccessful attempts.

Stopping devices

Smaller engines are usually stopped by closing the fuel cut-off valve on the injection pump via a cable, usually ending in a pull handle in the cockpit. Larger engines may use a solenoid-operated fuel cut-off valve,

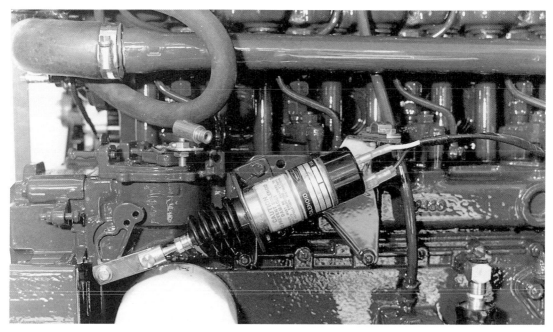

Small engines are often stopped by simply pulling a cable attached to the fuel shut-off valve. This engine has a solenoid-activated mechanism which performs the same function but is operated by a switch on the control panel.

operated by a switch fitted in the control panel. Electrical failure of the switch, solenoid or system means that the engine cannot be stopped, so an emergency pull wire, rope or cable should be fitted.

Fuel cleanliness

Fuel, even direct from the supplier, is never completely free of impurities. All fuels and lubricating oils are contaminated to some degree. Manufacturers supply fuels to international standards, but impurities can be introduced both in its handling and storage and in the boat's fuel system itself.

Fuel supplied to marine retail outlets is normally gas oil, dyed to distinguish it from automotive diesel (DERV), which is manufactured to a higher specification. This is not normally a problem, but if you have

any doubt about your engine's ability to run on marine diesel, refer to the manufacturer.

Fuel quality

Gas oil is supplied in the UK to BS2869 A2 & D, automotive diesel to BS EN 590:1993. It is manufactured and supplied to two temperature standards:

1. For use in temperatures above 0°C.
2. For use in temperatures above –8°C.
The first is delivered to retail outlets between mid-March to end September, the second between October and mid-March.

Gas oil in other countries could be manufactured to a different specification. If possible choose well-known brands, or buy automotive diesel.

A high sulphur content in fuel can cause severe problems inside the engine. Good quality lubricating oils have an alkaline additive which counteracts the acidic compounds formed in the combustion process, but may need changing more often. If the fuel smells of rotten eggs the sulphur content is high.

Water content can be tested by heating a small amount of fuel in a metal container. As the fuel heats up it will start to crackle. A loud crackle indicates a high water content, in which case the fuel should not be used.

Good fuel housekeeping

Most contamination is introduced after the fuel has left the pump. Keep the area surrounding the filler cap and the cap itself clean. Keep water out of the tank and every five years or so clean it out completely, or use a pump to empty out the last 10 to 15 litres at the bottom of the tank, where water will collect. When the boat is laid up in winter, keep the tank full to reduce the air gap and reduce condensation.

Always clean new parts scrupulously before fitting. Change the fine filter elements in accordance with the manufacturer's instructions, or each time the lubricating oil filter is changed – between 100 and 200 hours.

All fittings in the fuel system are sealed by either metal-to-metal seals or rubber-to-metal. Don't use PTFE tape or jointing compound. Debris entering the system will jam or block critical parts. Many engine manufacturers specify the tightening torque for important fittings. Do not exceed the recommendations.

To avoid fuel sloppping about and becoming aerated, or drawing air into the system,

keep the fuel tank well topped up. About 20 per cent is the lowest amount that should be allowed as a reserve.

It is essential to avoid water getting into the fuel tank, as a water trap can only cope with small quantities. Any air in the tank will contain some water, which will condense and form drops. Since water is heavier than fuel the water accumulates at the bottom of the tank.

Microbiological contamination

Water in the bottom of fuel tanks can be colonised by micro-organisms which live in the water and feed off the fuel. Given favourable breeding conditions these can multiply and block the fuel filters with a slimy debris, starving the engine of fuel and leading to poor performance. The organisms can also corrode the bottom of the tank, causing leaks.

The organisms can cause cloudiness in the fuel. The best method of treatment is to drain the tank and clean it. Then drain and clean the water trap and filter, and change the filter element. Refill with clean fuel and add a biocide to kill any surviving micro-organisms. Treat the fuel with biocide at least once a season.

Finally, remember that the problems most likely to cause your engine to stop, the ones responsible for more rescue call-outs than any other, are air or water in the fuel. Take special care to ensure the fuel in the tank is clean at the start of the season or after a long lay-up. Filters are often clogged by sediment from the tank, agitated in rough weather. Then, when you most need your engine, it fails you.

3 Air

Engines need even more air than they do fuel, so if the intake is restricted, the engine will run badly, stopping without apparent reason or producing black smoke.

The challenge is to keep sea water out of the engine compartment while allowing enough air in to feed the combustion process – conflicting requirements in rough weather. The compromise is generally to have large diameter pipes running from ducts set high in the cockpit area and covered by louvres.

An inlet cleaner – either a simple gauze strainer in a housing or a paper element similar to a car air cleaner – is normally fitted to trap debris being drawn into the engine. Strainer-type filters need to be cleaned once per season, paper elements changed according to the manufacturer's recommendations or at the same time as the fine fuel filters.

Turbochargers

Naturally aspirated engines rely on atmospheric pressure at around 1013 millibars to force air into the cylinders during the suction strokes of the pistons. Restrictions caused by inlet valves and manifold passages during natural aspiration mean that a full charge of air is never achieved.

Turbochargers boost this pressure to make up the deficiency. A turbocharger is a

To change the air filter on this engine, first unclip the cover then remove the filter. Wash it in soapy water, and dry thoroughly before replacing it. Check the wire mesh for disintegration and throw away if damaged.

Turbochargers are driven by the exhaust gases and force more air into the cylinders, resulting in higher engine output.

This air filter is of the paper element, disposable kind and cannot be washed out and reused. To replace it, simply unscrew the filter housing. The filter can be checked by shining a bright light through from the inside. Any clogged areas will show up immediately.

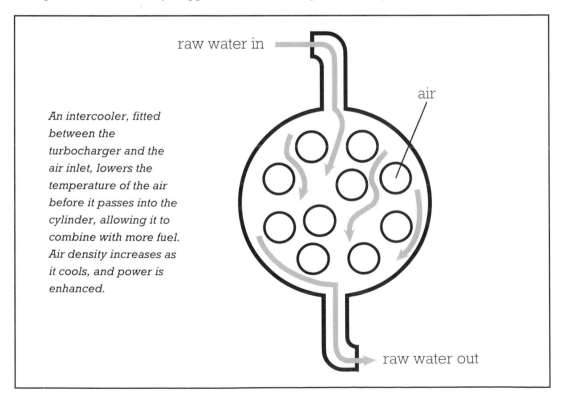

raw water in

air

An intercooler, fitted between the turbocharger and the air inlet, lowers the temperature of the air before it passes into the cylinder, allowing it to combine with more fuel. Air density increases as it cools, and power is enhanced.

raw water out

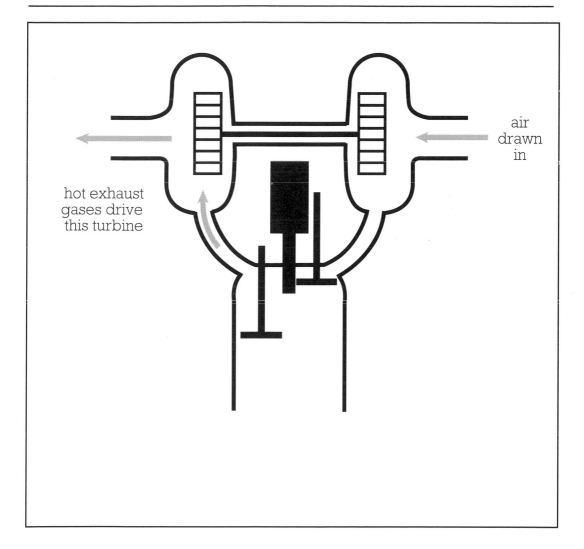

air
drawn
in

hot exhaust
gases drive
this turbine

turbine driven by the exhaust gases which in turn drives another turbine (see diagram). This forces air to the engine at a pressure higher than atmospheric, which means that even higher pressure can be generated during the power stroke. This results in higher output torque and increased engine output power.

As the exhaust runs at a high temperature, the materials used in the construction of the turbocharger need to be of a very high quality. Adequate lubrication of the bearings is essential and only high quality engine oil is normally specified for turbocharged engines.

Intercooler

Air density increases as its pressure increases and as its temperature is reduced. To get the maximum benefit from a turbocharger, an intercooler, or aftercooler, is sometimes fitted between the turbo and the engine air inlet. Fed with raw water, it cools the air entering the engine and enhances its power even further.

4 Cooling

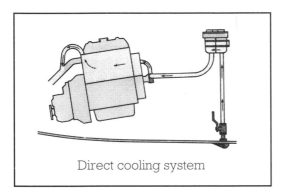

Direct cooling system

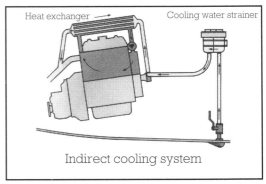

Heat exchanger — Cooling water strainer

Indirect cooling system

The temperature of combustion in a diesel engine is around ten times the temperature required for the moving parts to operate efficiently. Uncooled, an engine will rapidly lose power and may seize up completely.

Three types of cooling system are used to prevent this happening. Each has its advantages for certain types of boat. Air cooling, for instance, was extensively used on working canal boats where water inlets were vulnerable to blockage by weed, simplicity was of the essence and noise unlikely to cause a problem.

The systems are:
1. Air cooling.
2. Direct raw water cooling.
3. Indirect water cooling.

Air cooling
The main advantage of air cooling is that there is no water to corrode the engine's internals. A disadvantage is that the engine needs a large amount of air around it to keep it at a reasonable temperature. The running temperature is also difficult to control. Air-cooled engines are also very noisy compared with water-cooled ones, which accounts for their declining popularity now that canals are used more for relaxation than for work.

Direct (raw-water) cooling
This is generally used on smaller engines. The engine is cooled by raw water drawn directly from outside of the boat. It is pumped through the water passages in the engine, into the exhaust pipe and exits through the exhaust. A simple system, it has a slight advantage in that sea water is less likely to freeze in the block and cause damage than fresh water (although beware, it will freeze if the air temperature is cold enough). The main drawback is that the internal waterways will in time corrode and fill with salt deposits and other debris. A major strip-down and overhaul is then required.

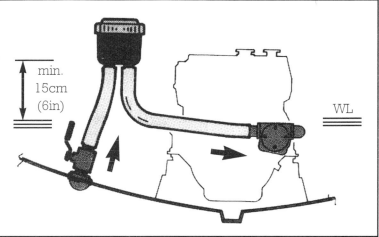

This Vetus water strainer will effectively trap any debris entering the cooling system. It should be fitted at least 15cm (6in) above the waterline for safety in case any of the pipe unions are leaky.

Indirect cooling

This uses a separate engine cooling water circuit, together with a heat exchanger. The engine cooling water – fresh water with antifreeze and corrosion inhibitors added – is pumped through the engine. Raw water flows without restriction through the heat exchanger, drawing heat from the engine cooling water and from the exhaust as well on its way back overboard.

The temperature of indirect-cooled engines can generally be regulated better because the flow around the engine is controlled by a thermostat. This control allows the engine to run at a higher temperature than its raw-water cooled counterpart. Furthermore the fresh water system does not accumulate debris or salts and can easily be drained, flushed and refilled, so no major strip-down is needed. Always use de-ionised water in the fresh water system.

The majority of steel inland waterway boats use a system called 'keel' cooling. Here the engine cooling water is circulated through a cooling tank which is part of the hull below the waterline. No raw water is needed to cool the engine, so there are no problems with mud, debris and weeds.

Inlet valves

Several types are used, all normally connected directly to the inlet skin fitting. They enable the water to be turned off when the boat is left and for maintenance purposes. The most common are:

1. Gate valves, which have a sliding plate to open or close the flow passage through the valve. They are inclined to stiffen unless used frequently.
2. Ball valves, which use a ball shape with a hole through it. When turned to line the hole up with the inlet and outlet passages, water passes through. The handle is simply turned through 90° and it is easy to see whether the valve is open or closed: if the handle is in line with the pipe, the valve is open.
3. Cone valves are similar in principle to ball valves except that the sealing element is a cone with a hole through it. When the cone is turned through 90° it opens a passageway through the valve.

Debris seen through the transparent cover on this water strainer will restrict water flow and may cause overheating. To clear it, unbolt the cover, remove the strainer and wash it out.

Water strainer

This mesh strainer can be incorporated in the inlet valve or sited separately to keep debris from entering the system.

Separate water strainer

Mounted about 150mm above the waterline these normally have clear plastic covers so that contamination can be seen and water flow monitored while the engine is running. The strainer element can be removed for cleaning, but not while the engine is running unless a duplicate strainer is fitted.

Water pipes

A pipe of too small a bore will restrict the flow of water to the engine.

At least part of the pipe between the inlet valve fitted to the hull and the pump mounted on the engine must be flexible to allow for engine vibration. Use two hose clips for security at each end of the pipe, and make it long enough to allow plenty of movement of the engine without imposing strains on the pipe and inlet valve.

Special water hose is manufactured from a different material from fuel hoses and will not be chemically affected by the water. Garden hose-type piping should not be used as it has a tendency to kink, reducing the flow area and causing inadequate water flow and overheating: genuine water hose is reinforced with a spiral steel inlay to prevent this. The hose should be insulated and fire resistant to a point above the waterline.

Water pumps

Early pumps were generally reciprocating piston types, driven by an eccentric cam from the engine. They are rarely found on

The water system should be plumbed using non-kink, large-bore water piping, long enough to soak up any engine movement, ideally double jubilee-clipped. The picture shows a Vetus strainer and Jabsco-type water pump.

modern engines, most of which have rotary pumps with a rubber impeller.

Piston pumps

Grease piston pumps regularly via the greaser cup. It may occasionally be necessary to inspect the non-return valves.

Impeller pumps

These have a rubber bladed impeller (normally neoprene) rotating inside a round housing which has a depression machined between the inlet and outlet ports. The pump is driven directly by the engine. As the impeller rotates water is drawn in on the inlet side of the depression, and the blades carry it around until they

Neoprene impellers fitted to water pumps are reliable, unless run dry or allowed to become damaged by sand or debris. Use a dab of Vaseline to lubricate the replacement.

The thermostat regulates cooling water flow, opening and closing depending on engine heat, allowing more or less water to pass, thus keeping engine temeperature stable. Thermostats cannot be repaired.

reach the outlet side. Check valves are not required as the pumping action is continuous.

The effectiveness of the pump depends on the impeller fitting closely in the housing, which is why it tends to overheat and fail if allowed to run dry.

If the engine is laid up for a while, for example over the winter, the impeller should be removed and checked for damage before the engine is used again. Even if it looks good, but has had plenty of use, replace it anyway and always keep a service kit including an impeller and gasket on board.

The easiest way to remove an impeller is with a slipjoint wrench (water pump pliers, preferably old ones with rounded teeth). Using screwdrivers is difficult and can

damage the impeller, and the mating face of the pump.

Always apply light grease or petroleum jelly to both the impeller and the pump housing to enable it to run without problems until water starts passing through. Impellers impregnated with lubricant to withstand dry running for several minutes are now available to fit most pumps.

A rubber seal behind the pump body stops water leaking out down the shaft., while a similar seal on the engine side stops oil leaking the other way. The gap between the two seals has a small drain hole. Should either water or oil be leaking from the hole the appropriate seal needs to be changed. If a water leak is left indefinitely a salt deposit will build up around the drain hole.

Thermostat

An engine should be run at its designated operating temperature for best performance. The thermostat keeps the cooling water temperature in the correct range, sensing the water temperature in

The most common type of exhaust – and safest in terms of fire risk – is the wet exhaust, where cooling water is injected into the pipe at the manifold But beware backflow into the engine.

the engine and responding by opening or closing, allowing water to circulate when the temperature rises, and preventing circulation when the temperature falls. The thermostat is basically a cylinder filled with wax which expands as the temperature rises. At a set point the valve opens to allow flow into the engine water cooling passages. A hole in the thermostat bypasses the valve and allows a small amount of flow at all times.

The opening temperature of a thermostat is normally marked on it. For raw-water cooled engines this will be between 45-50°C, for indirect cooled engines 79-85°C.

A thermostat can be tested by immersing it in hot water, and checking the temperature at which the valve opens against the temperature of the water as shown by a thermometer.

It is not possible to adjust or repair a thermostat. If it doesn't work properly it needs to be replaced. If it is jammed closed and the engine is overheating it can be removed and the engine run without it, albeit cooler than its designed temperature.

It may not be obvious in which direction a thermostat works, so check the service manual. If it is put in the wrong way round it will not open and the engine will overheat.

Exhaust systems

The conventional wet exhaust is a purpose-made flexible reinforced rubber tube connected to the exhaust manifold on the engine and usually terminating at the transom. The cooling water from the engine

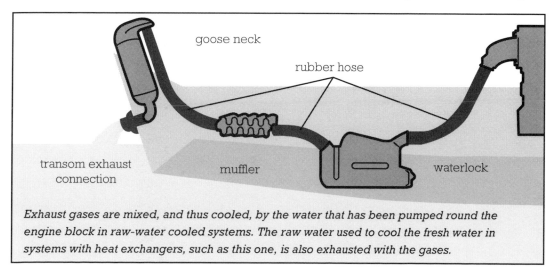

Exhaust gases are mixed, and thus cooled, by the water that has been pumped round the engine block in raw-water cooled systems. The raw water used to cool the fresh water in systems with heat exchangers, such as this one, is also exhausted with the gases.

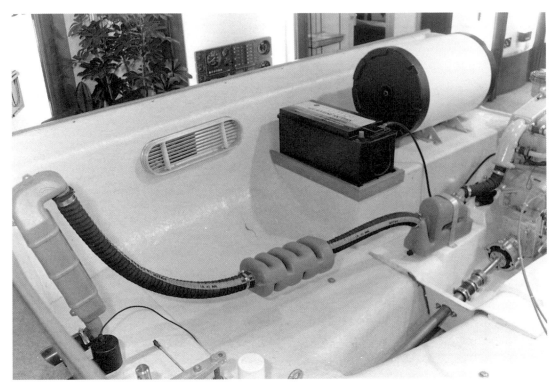

A Vetus exhaust system in place on a mocked-up boat, showing clearly the swan neck (or goose neck) in the foreground, muffler and waterlock or trap.

or heat exchanger is injected into the exhaust manifold outlet, cooling the exhaust pipe, before exiting along with the exhaust gases.

Having water in the exhaust can lead to backflow into the engine, with consequent damage. Safeguards include an anti-syphon device, a water trap and a swan or goose neck.

Anti-syphon device

This device stops water syphoning back up the exhaust pipe into the engine. It should be sited so that the outlet pipe or non-return valve is at least 300mm (12in) above the waterline – essential if the point at which the water is injected into the exhaust is less than 150mm (6in) above the waterline.

Anti-syphon devices are optional extras on many installations, but are worth the added expense because of the consequences of backflow.

Water trap

This is a chamber to collect any water that remains in the exhaust pipe when the engine is stopped. It also acts as a baffle and silencer. Made of GRP, plastic or stainless steel, it must be positioned below the engine exhaust outlet, at the lowest point of the exhaust system, so that water can drain to it.

A plastic water trap can melt if the engine is run without cooling water. This can result in exhaust fumes collecting in the boat, heat build up and possibly fire. An exhaust

If the engine is overheating check that the cooling water intake valve is open – handle in line with the pipe. It is vital to lag the pipe in case of an engine fire.

The header tank level needs to be checked periodically and filled to finger level. The system is flushed by opening the drain tap on the engine block, letting the water/antifreeze mix drain into the bilge.

temperature alarm sensor can be fitted to the trap to indicate loss of water flow. GRP and stainless steel water traps will withstand higher temperatures.

Swan or goose neck

Water forced into the exhaust by following seas can have catastrophic effects. The exhaust tube should be formed into a swan neck before it exits from the boat, with the top of the neck routed as high above the waterline as possible. An exhaust non-return valve could be fitted near the skin fitting as an alternative or additional precaution.

Heat exchangers

Heat exchangers are used with indirect cooling systems. The hot engine (fresh) cooling water passes over a stack of pipes containing raw water, which absorbs the heat and carries it away. The engine cooling water flows in the opposite direction to the raw water.

Heat exchangers can be serviced by dismantling them and cleaning the parts. In

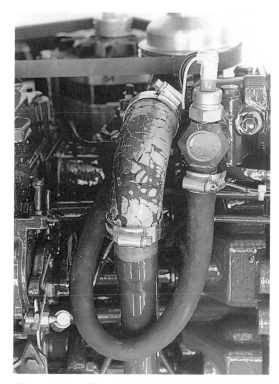

Hose pipes will crack after a time, and lead to overheating in an indirect system. Replace them after four or five years. Note the temperature sensor wire at the top right.

particular the raw-water flow channels may need cleaning, so long as care is taken not to damage the tubes when rodding.

Leaks

If a leak is detected between the raw water and freshwater systems, it is most likely to be in the heat exchanger. The seals between the two systems may need to be renewed, tightened etc. This is a water system, so jointing compound or gaskets can be used with no problems.

A leak will be apparent if water drips from the freshwater overflow pipe when the engine is running. This pipe is usually fitted to the side of the filler cap on the header tank, and exits under the engine. The pipe can be removed from the cap to check for any leaks.

Direct cooling systems

Leaks in raw water systems can cause extensive engine corrosion so they should be cured as soon as possible.

Rubber pipes deteriorate with age and lose both flexibility and elasticity. Temporary repairs to hoses can be carried out with insulation tape and a hose clip.

Heavy duty hose clamps are available in larger sizes and provide an even pressure around the hose. Include in any maintenance programme replacement of hoses and clamps after five or six years.

Most direct-cooled engines have a sacrificial zinc anode to minimise corrosion, fitted somewhere inside the engine block. This should be checked annually and renewed if more than 50% eroded.

Indirect cooling systems

Any water leakage from an indirect system will cause overheating when the level gets low enough. Replace hoses every five or six years and check the condition of brass and steel plated fittings, which can deteriorate through electrolysis and are liable to crack if overtightened.

Internal leaks into the engine will contaminate the lubricating oil and seriously damage the engine if left unattended. See Chapter 9.

Sealing materials

PTFE tape can be used with care to seal threaded connections. Jointing compound is also acceptable to improve sealing under hose clips. Apply the compound to the pipe, however, not the inside of the hose, to avoid scraping it off into the system.

5 Lubrication

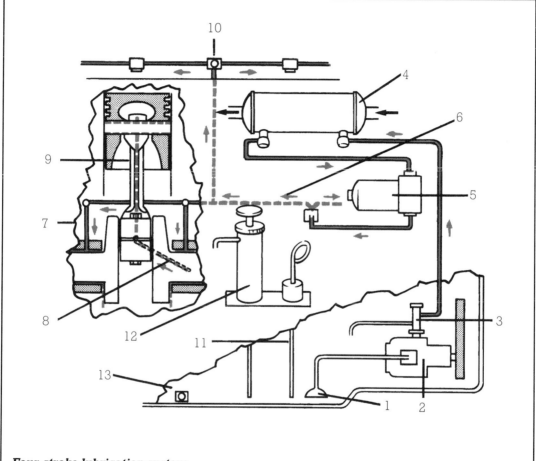

Four-stroke lubrication system

1 Oil strainer. 2 Oil pump. 3 Pressure release valve. 4 Oil cooler. 5 Oil filter.
6 Oil gallery. 7 Oil feed to main bearing. 8 Oil feed through crankshaft to big end bearing.
9 Oil feed through connecting rod to small end bush and gudgeon pin.
10 Oil feed to valve gear. 11 Dipstick. 12 Sump pump. 13 Sump drain plug.

Lubricating oil acts as a barrier between moving parts, reducing wear. It is normally distributed around the engine by means of a pump before being returned to the sump.

In some slow running engines lubrication is by 'splash'. With this system, as the name implies, oil is thrown to the bearings, bores etc as the engine turns over.

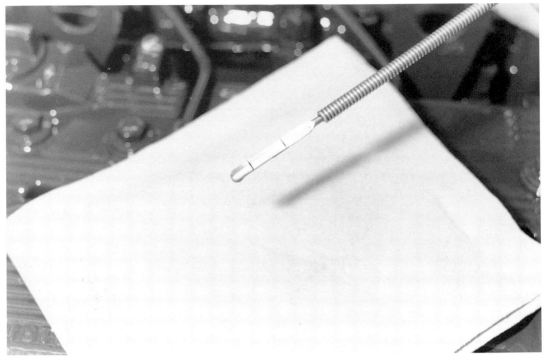

Keep the oil level between the marks on the dipstick. The colour of the lubricating oil in the system says much for the engine's health and can be analysed for evidence of internal wear. Diesel lubricating oil becomes black through the action of its additives. Grey means water is present.

In a pumped system the oil normally flows to the bearings etc through holes either cast or drilled into the engine casing.

The lubricating oil level in the engine should always be kept within the limits marked on the dipstick.

Pumps

Constant displacement pumps are continuously driven from the engine, their output depending on engine speed. The internal parts of the pump are machined to fine tolerances and use very close fitting parts. Any scoring or wear will harm their efficiency. This will become apparent if the pressure generated at low speed is insufficient to operate the pressure switch or fails to meet the manufacturer's recommended minimum pressure.

Suction strainer

Fitted primarily to protect the pump from sucking in stray nuts and bolts, the strainer is sited low down in the sump and connected to the pump by a steel pipe.

Relief valve

Oil pressure in an engine is determined by the resistance to flow, and limited by a factory-set relief valve. This is a spring-loaded plunger which lifts to allow oil to bypass the system and flow directly from the outlet of the pump to the inlet or to the sump when the setting is reached. If debris jams this relief valve open, oil will bypass continuously and the working pressure will not be reached.

Oil filter

The filter ensures that the oil reaching the moving parts and bearings is clean. The quality of filtration is determined by the engine manufacturer.

Filter cartridges may incorporate reverse flow non-return valves and a bypass in case the filter becomes clogged, set to operate at a specific pressure. Only manufacturer's recommended spares should be used.

The non-return valve stops oil draining out of the bearings back into the sump when the engine is stopped, and thereby ensures that pressure builds up promptly when the engine is started.

Lubricating oil washes the engine parts and collects debris. Most of this will settle in the sump but fine particles will remain suspended in the oil and pass through the pump to be collected by the filter.

The filter element should be changed whenever the lubricating oil is changed. All engines in current production use spin-on filter cartridges, which can be removed easily with a chain or strap wrench.

It may be possible to undo a cartridge by hand: if a two-handed grip is possible wrap a piece of emery paper around the cartridge to provide a better grip. Another solution is to fit a large hose clip around it and tap round with a hammer.

Fill the new cartridge with fresh oil. Then, making sure that the rubber sealing element is in place, screw on until the sealing ring is compressed, and tighten by hand using the emery paper to provide a better grip.

Before restarting the engine, turn it over by hand or on the starter motor with the fuel pump engine stop valve closed to circulate the new oil around the engine and fill the filter and passages. Check and tighten the filter after running the engine.

Lubricating oil

The oil used for lubrication is a sophisticated product, and some diesels require a higher specification oil than that used for petrol engines. The reasons for this are:

1. Working pressures are higher in diesel engines.
2. Running temperatures can be higher.
3. Chemical conditions imposed by the combustion process are more severe.

In an oil developed for diesel engines the basic oil content is about 75 per cent, with additives making up the balance. These include:

1. Detergents to keep the inside of the engine clean.
2. Anti-wear additives to extend the life of wearing parts, particularly the valve gear.
3. Oxidation inhibitors which reduce the rate at which the oil base deteriorates when used.
4. Anti foam agents.
5. Viscosity index improvers to keep the oil fluid at low temperatures and thick at high temperatures.
6. Alkaline additives to counteract acidic compounds formed by the diesel combustion process.
7. Anti rust agents for engine protection.

There are various systems of classifying lubricating oils for viscosity. The common

How to change the oil

1. Run the engine up to operating temperature and stop.

2. Drain the engine oil through the sump plug into a container, or pump oil out through the dipstick tube using the hand pump if fitted. If you use a separate pump, push the tube down until you feel it touch the bottom of the sump.

3. Remove the old oil filter, fill the new one with engine oil and fit as tight as you can by hand, first smearing some oil on the rubber sealing ring.

4. Fill the engine with clean oil to the correct dipstick level.

5. Run engine, stop, check the oil level again, and retighten the filter.

   IMPORTANT. Waste or spilled oil should always be disposed of in designated receptacles ashore, never in the sea, river or canal.

Gearbox

Some engines share their lubricating oil with the gearbox, in others the two systems are separate. In the clutch-type gearbox the normal lubrication recommended is Automatic Transmission Fluid, or ATF.

In all cases refer either to the engine manufacturer or the gearbox manufacturer for the fluid recommended.

Heat is generated in the gearbox through the end loading imposed by the propeller shaft on the bearings, and where high powers are being transmitted the oil needs to be cooled. This is usually achieved with a heat exchanger cooled by water from the raw water engine cooling system.

Always use clean gearbox oil, as there are no filters incorporated in the system. Fill to the recommended level shown on the dipstick or the fill plug. Be careful, also, not to lose the plastic fill pipe often supplied with the plastic oil container; it will invariably disappear into the gearbox. A funnel is the answer.

ones are SAE (US Society of Automotive Engineers). A typical specification would be either SAE 10W30 for low temperature applications or SAE 15W40 for summer temperatures.

The standard method of specifying the quality of diesel engine lubricating oils is the API (American Petroleum Institute)

reference CA to CE, API CE being the highest quality. The SA to SG range is for petrol engines.

European quality standards are defined by the CCMC (Comité des Constructeurs d'Automobiles du Marché Commun), a typical European engine oil being D4 or D5, or for passenger cars PD2. D5 is for

*Changing the oil (clockwise from top left).
1. Using the built-in pump to change the oil,
typically about a gallon for a 30hp engine.
2. A strap wrench makes easy work of
removing the oil filter. Alternatively, and
messier, spear the filter with a screw-driver
and twist. 3. A plastic bag will catch most
of the leaks. A smear of oil will help bed
the new filter. 4 and 5. After filling and
running the engine, recheck oil level and
top up if necessary. Dispose of oil and
filter responsibly.*

Super High Performance Diesels.

Oils to a higher classification are generally
suitable for applications of a lower class.
Always refer to the engine manufacturer's
instructions for both the viscosity grades
and the minimum quality required. Some
manufacturers recommend standard auto
oil for both engine and gearbox and have
developed their own products.

Mixing oils

Engine lubricating oils are designed to be
mixable with oils of a different standard.

The gearbox will have a separate dipstick and may well share the same grade of oil as the engine. Gearbox oil is not filtered during use. It not only lubricates the gears but cools the box, often along with a water jacket.

Engines cover a wide range of service conditions from low powered, lightly loaded applications to heavily loaded applications using high powered turbo engines. The specification of lubricating oils reflects the service conditions, for example the more taxing the service the higher the specification of oil required.

Naturally aspirated engines, particularly those operating in lightly loaded applications, may need a lower grade oil for running in, to bed in the bores and avoid bore polishing which can result in high lubricating oil consumption. Consult the manufacturer for recommendations

when running in a new or reconditioned engine.

Where a high sulphur content fuel is used, the lubricating oil should be changed more frequently.

Oil companies can provide an oil analysis service which can determine wear rates and combustion efficiency.

In the writer's experience it is difficult to buy anything but high grade car diesel lubricating oil at automobile filling stations and oil suppliers are always in large towns miles away from the coast or any marinas.

If a long trip is planned take at least enough oil and spare filters for as many changes as you expect to make and avoid any anxiety caused by exceeding the recommended change interval or using oil that you are unsure of.

Waste oil and the oily water found in the bilges should never be disposed of in the sea or inland waterways. As well as damaging the environment, this is illegal and could result in a heavy fine. Most marinas offer disposal facilities, and these should be used.

Health

It is good practice to avoid skin contact with mineral oils. Used diesel oil has deposits in it formed during combustion which are potentially harmful. Wear protective gloves when changing either oil or filters.

6 Electrical systems

Although a diesel does not have an electrical ignition system, any electric-start model – which means the majority – still needs to produce electricity to run the starter motor when required, and supply on board services such as lights.As well as the starter motor, therefore, there is a requirement for an alternator to produce the electricity, a battery to store it, and a number of control units. We will begin, appropriately, with the starting system.

Starter motor and relay

The starting system comprises two components, the motor itself and its solenoid-operated electrical relay.

The relay is necessary because the heavy electrical currents delivered to the starter motor by the battery are too large for the key-type starter switch to carry. When the key is moved to its spring-loaded start position, the relay solenoid closes the large

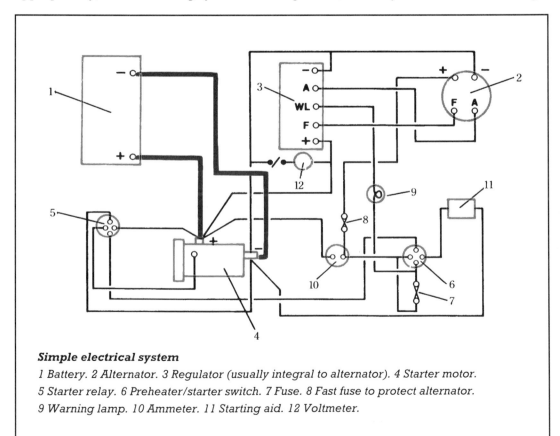

Simple electrical system

1 Battery. 2 Alternator. 3 Regulator (usually integral to alternator). 4 Starter motor.
5 Starter relay. 6 Preheater/starter switch. 7 Fuse. 8 Fast fuse to protect alternator.
9 Warning lamp. 10 Ammeter. 11 Starting aid. 12 Voltmeter.

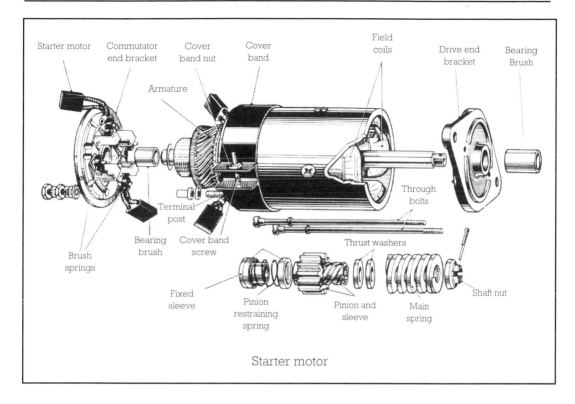

Starter motor

contacts, connecting the batteries directly to the motor.

As the motor starts to turn, the drive pinion on the output shaft is thrown outwards towards the ring gear on the engine flywheel. The pinion and ring gear have shaped teeth which allow the pinion to engage easily. The output shaft of the starter motor picks up speed and turns the engine.

As soon as the engine fires, the start switch is allowed to return to the run position. The ring gear accelerates, the pinion is thrown out of contact with the ring gear by a spring and the starter motor stops.

If the engine is particularly quiet, you may not be aware it is running, so watch the instrumentation. Never engage the starter while the engine is running as the gears may be damaged beyond repair.

Another type of starter motor has the pinion engaging with the ring gear before the electrical connection is made. Again it is thrown out of contact when the engine picks up and when the starter switch is returned to the run position.

The electrical resistance of starter motors is extremely small and it is impossible to check accurately with a multimeter if the resistance is correct or not. If there is an electrical problem, the motor needs to be taken to a specialist.

Starter motor wiring

The current passing through starter motors is high and both the positive and negative cables from the battery need to be large

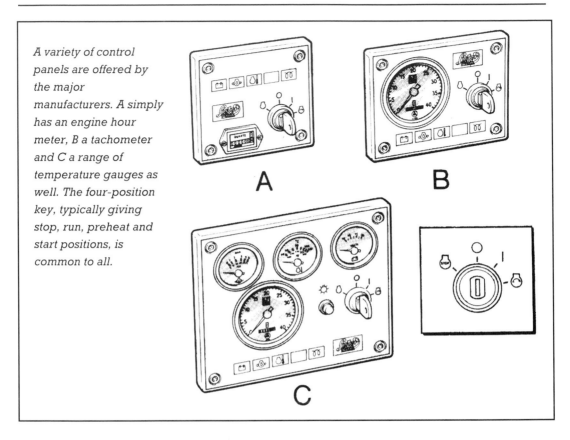

A variety of control panels are offered by the major manufacturers. A simply has an engine hour meter, B a tachometer and C a range of temperature gauges as well. The four-position key, typically giving stop, run, preheat and start positions, is common to all.

enough to carry the current with minimal loss of voltage. Both positive and negative terminals at the battery and the motor must be clean and secure.

Alternators

These generate electric power and are driven by the engine, usually through a V-belt or multi V-belt. The alternator normally runs faster than the engine, the speed ratio being determined by the diameters of the respective pulleys.

The drive belt should be neither too tight nor too slack. It should be possible to move the belt at its longest part by plus or minus 12mm (1/2in). A belt that is too tight will shorten the life of the bearings in the alternator, while a slack belt will provide

insufficient friction to transmit the power and the belt will slip, giving reduced speed. You can usually adjust the tension by rotating the alternator about its primary fixing point and locking it in position using the bolt in the slotted adjustment arm.

The alternator supplies alternating current (AC) which is converted into direct current (DC) by its own rectifiers and used primarily to charge the batteries. The batteries themselves, since they are accumulators, smooth the alternator output.

Regulation

The alternator constantly senses the output voltage and when a preset voltage is reached – usually 14.2 volts – will progressively shut itself down to supply just enough current to maintain that voltage.

It is possible to buy devices which sense battery condition and allow the alternator to push through a higher voltage, thereby ensuring faster charging. These are useful when the batteries are used a lot, but not the engine. Consult a specialist when considering this type of equipment.

Some alternators can be offloaded electrically at start up to reduce the load on the starter motor. The lubricating oil pressure switch is usually the agent for bringing the alternator onto load. When the oil pressure rises, the warning light goes off, simultaneously switching in the alternator.

Voltage sensing

If the sensing wire breaks or becomes disconnected the alternator will run at full output at all times. This will quickly cause the batteries to boil, produce potentially explosive gases and finally self-destruct. An amber light, usually installed in the engine control panel, goes out when the alternator is charging. A voltmeter and

ammeter will tell you what the output voltage and current are.

Engine speed

The alternator is often used to measure the engine speed which is then displayed on the tachometer. If the engine is running normally but the display indicates otherwise the alternator drive belt could be slipping.

Starter-generator

Many older marine engines use combined starter motors and generators. These have limited torque as starter motors, and the exhaust valve lifter may need to be used to reduce the compression, allowing the engine to spin with sufficient speed to fire.

Diesels don't need electricity to run, but an alternator will keep batteries charged to run services or feed the starter motor. A slipping belt will reduce alternator efficiency.

A voltmeter will show battery state at a glance, but not how long that state will last. Alternatively a multimeter can be used across the terminals of the battery selector switch.

The most common type of battery is still the lead-acid type. Capacity is given in amp hours (Ah): a 200Ah battery will give 10 amps for 20 hours. Truck batteries are adequate for starting purposes, while deep cycle or traction batteries which can be constantly charged and discharged are better for all-purpose use. Note that in this installation the battery is not secured. Batteries should be housed in a closed compartment – ideally in individual cases – and securely fixed to avoid spillage of acid. The compartment should be vented overboard to prevent build-up of hydrogen.

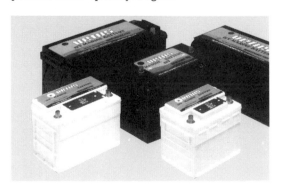

Once the engine is running the starter becomes a generator, but because it is a straight DC machine its output is limited. Output is controlled by a charging regulator.

The main drawback of these units is that they need to spin at medium to fast speed to generate sufficient power both to charge the batteries and to operate the boat's systems. If the electrical systems are designed to take this into account they work well.

Batteries

The number, size and type of batteries used on a boat will depend on the electrical power requirements both when the engine is running and when it is at rest. Managing power, and ensuring adequate charging, is as important to the yacht's electrical well-being as good fuel hygiene is to the engine's.

Truck batteries are ideal for starting a diesel as they will supply high currents to the starter motor when required. They are not so good, however, at supplying power over long periods for lights, equipment, pumps etc, and will have a limited life if continually drained and recharged. If they are kept fully charged, and the current drain between charging periods is modest, they will last a considerable time.

Deep cycle batteries are designed to supply power over a long period before being recharged. They are thus ideal for running the boat's services and can be combined with a truck battery for starting.

Battery maintenance

Lead acid batteries need their electrolyte to

be kept topped up above the plates with distilled water. Some batteries are sealed, which eliminates this requirement.

When the battery is fully charged a graduated hydrometer can be used to check the specific gravity of the electrolyte. An accurate digital multimeter will also give a good indication of the battery condition, the fully charged voltage being 12.6 volts.

Battery installation

Batteries give off hydrogen when charging and should be installed in a closed compartment, vented overboard. They must be firmly secured so that they cannot spill or move about.

Isolator switch

If the battery isolator, fitted for safety reasons, is also used to select different batteries it is essential that the second battery is switched in before the first is switched out. If not, and the engine is running, the alternator diodes can be damaged or destroyed during the period that both batteries are disconnected. For the same reasons never disconnect or swap the connections to another battery while the engine is running.

The switch needs to be man enough to offer little or no resistance to current flow

The isolator switch, here fitted with a disabling lock to protect the batteries, enables any combination of ship's batteries to be chosen.

when the starter motor is operating.

Mains chargers

To avoid the batteries discharging through leakage in a permanently fitted charger, the charger should be connected into the system on the boat side of the isolator switch. The battery to be charged can then be selected by using the isolator switch. Take care not to switch on the charger with the isolator switch in the off position.

7 Installation

A boat's engine and drive system must be precisely aligned to minimise wear and vibration. However, the most carefully installed drive system can go out of alignment when the boat is out of the water, when the hull can become distorted. Periodic checking, and careful investigation of any untoward vibration or noise, will pay dividends.

Flexible mounts

These comprise steel shells with rubber bonded between them, and insulate the hull from engine vibration. When choosing the correct size the torque and thrust from the propeller must be taken into account. Once fitted you should avoid spilling fuel or lubricating oil onto the rubber as it will in time soften and swell.

Alignment of the propeller shaft

Whether the engine is mated to its drive shaft by a flexible coupling or connected directly to the propeller shaft flange, it must be carefully aligned. The engine output must run both square and concentric with the mating propeller shaft flange.

Although shafts, couplings and flanges are

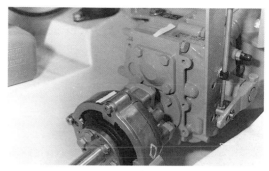

Perfect alignment between engine and shaft is difficult to achieve, but excessive misalignment will reduce bearing life.

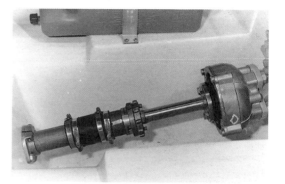

Engine mounts isolate vibration from the hull and allow the engine position to be adjusted for accurate alignment. The top nut is loosened and the lower nut turned to raise or lower the engine.

Various types of shaft seal are available, some water lubricated. This Vetus system will prevent water leakage into the hull and does not rely on a messy, grease-filled stuffing box.

machined to precise tolerances, perfect alignment is often difficult to achieve. Nevertheless, significant misalignment will result in excessive wear of the bearings. If the drive flange is not square the propeller shaft will vibrate, causing rapid wear of the bearings. Bent shafts and flanges should be repaired ashore.

Alignment of the engine is carried out by adjusting the engine mounting bolts for position and height, to achieve close contact on all parts of the connecting flanges. You can test for close contact by trying to insert a feeler gauge between the

Tightening the flange bolts on this old-fashioned stuffing box compresses a fibre wadding and, together with a gland greaser, will prevent most leaks around the shaft. Overtightening will damage the shaft.

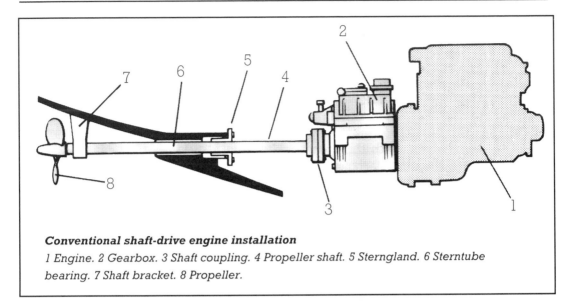

Conventional shaft-drive engine installation
1 Engine. 2 Gearbox. 3 Shaft coupling. 4 Propeller shaft. 5 Sterngland. 6 Sterntube bearing. 7 Shaft bracket. 8 Propeller.

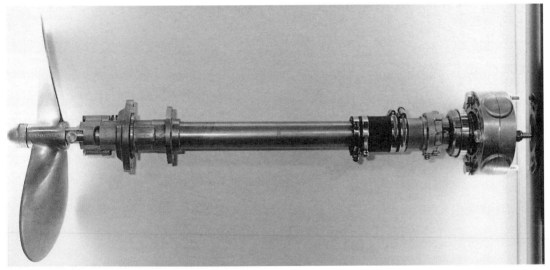

A typical Vetus sterngear set-up showing a two-bladed propeller, bearing, stern gland and flange.

flanges. The flanges must also be aligned, up and down and sideways.

Adjustments are made by moving the engine up or down using the lower nuts on the extended threaded rods on top of the engine mounts. When the engine is finally aligned, tighten the top nuts and use a lock washer.

Saildrive units are self-aligning, but the mountings still need to be properly set up to spread the loads correctly over the hull.

Flexible drive couplings

Unless it is specifically designed to allow an angular misalignment, you must take the same care lining up a flexible coupling and its engine. This will extend the life of the

This three-bladed powerboat propeller and shaft runs in a water-lubricated cutless bearing, supported in a bronze P bracket.

coupling, the gearbox bearings and the shaft bearings.

Shaft seals

Conventional seals consist of a stuffing box into which are laid several layers of grease-impregnated packing specifically made for the purpose. The box is closed by tightening the bolts in the outer flange. This compresses the packing, causing it to seal against the shaft.

The flange needs to be tightened just enough to stop leaks. If you overtighten the bolts, the result will be heat and wear on the shaft, possibly causing twisting and failure of the rubber sleeve which connects it to the stern tube.

The flange should be retightened as soon as a leak is seen. If leaks are persistent change the packing. Some stuffing boxes have external greasers so that grease can be injected after or during use.

Rubber lip seals are also used, similar to those in the engine, to seal in oil around a shaft, but made from a material compatible with water.

Face seals are becoming increasingly popular. They work by mating a precisely ground stainless steel face against a carbon face. Rubber gaiters hose-clipped to their respective shaft and stern tube both provide flexibility and spring the faces together.

Face seals may need special lubrication procedures during launch and initial start up, so refer to the manufacturers for instructions.

Propellers

Propellers need to be balanced to run smoothly. Any imbalance caused by chipped blades or other damage will produce vibration and reduce bearing and gearbox life.

Propeller shaft support bearings

To keep the shaft aligned, and provide support, its is held by two sets of bearings – one supporting the gearbox, fixed inside the boat, and the other either in the sternpost or in a P or A bracket extending from the hull.

The bearings in the gearbox or the boat provide both thrust and radial support. The outer bearing provides only radial support. The outer bearing is normally of the cutless type in which the shaft turns inside a rubber sleeve, grooved to assist water lubrication and bonded to a bronze outer sleeve.

Some internal bearings need a supply of water to keep them lubricated, in which case a feed line will have to be plumbed in.

Engine compartment

An engine compartment must not only let in sufficient air to feed the engine, but also keep out any sea water that threatens to disable the engine. A single cupful of water in the inlet manifold will disable and ruin an engine, putting at risk both the boat and the lives of the crew.

The engine must also be protected against water filling the cockpit and pouring through the main hatch in bad weather. Engine covers and access doors must be secured against water entry.

Engine compartments need to be insulated against both noise and fire for safety and comfort. You can buy a range of lead-lined, foam insulating materials for this.

The engine compartment should be kept free of all wiring except that required by the engine. Everything else should be run externally or, if that is impractical, insulated against the effects of an engine fire.

8 Gearboxes

The term 'gearbox' is misleadingly simple, covering as it does one of the more complex parts of an engine. In most installations the box in question serves three functions: to connect the engine to the propeller shaft, to provide reverse gear, and to reduce the drive speed from the engine.

Gear ratios and propellers

Large propellers provide a high degree of bite and control at low speeds but high drag when sailing. Small propellers have less drag but also less control for slow speed manoeuvring, and are inefficient at normal speeds.

The optimum choice of shaft speed and propeller depends on the displacement, type, length and shape of the boat. A typical propeller for a 25ft long keel displacement yacht might be 14 x 9, three-bladed. The first figure is the diameter in inches, the second a measure of the pitch or coarseness of the blades. This is the length, again measured in inches, of an imaginary cylinder of water drawn through the propeller in the course of a single revolution.

For yachts the engine speed is normally too high to drive the propeller directly so a ratio of between 1.5:1 and 3:1 is normally used. This means that for every 1.5 or 3 times the engine turns, the propeller turns once. Planing powerboats may have smaller ratios, displacement powerboats higher ratios.

There are three main types of gearbox:

1. Helical gears with clutch.
2. Epicyclic.
3. Cone clutch.

Helical gears

A helical gearbox incorporates two multi-disc clutches and two gear trains terminating in the output shaft. One clutch is engaged for forward, the other for reverse. Because of the action of the gears rotating in the lubricating oil, helical gearboxes tend to run hot. Large gearboxes or those working in unusual circumstances therefore need oil coolers.

No adjustment is needed as the clutches are self compensating for wear. It is, however, important to ensure that full movement is obtained when the control arm is engaged so as to avoid clutch slip.

The lubricating oil specified for helical gearboxes is usually Automotive Transmission Fluid (ATF). Under no circumstances deviate from the manufacturer's specifications.

Epicyclic gearboxes

Epicyclic gearboxes use a sun and planet gear train which reverses when the outer gear is restrained (see diagram below). The engagement adjustment needs to be positive to avoid slippage and the manufacturer's recommendations regarding lubrication must be followed closely.

Cone clutch gearboxes

Cone clutch-type gearboxes incorporate two gear trains, similar to the helical gearbox. The cones work as clutches when the male and female parts are forced

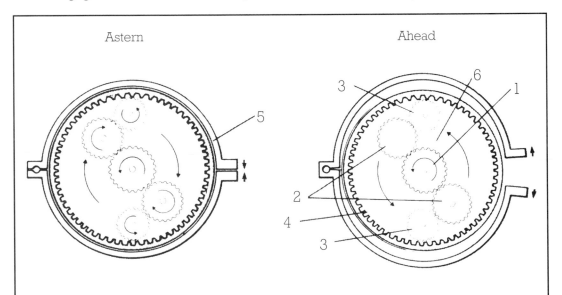

Epicyclic gearboxes use a sun and planet gear train which reverses when the outer gear is restrained. Ahead is depicted on the right and astern on the left. 1 Drive or sun gear. 2 Pinion gears. 3 Spur gears. 4 Annulus with internal gear teeth. 5 Brake band shown locked in astern position. 6 Assembly which carries pinion and spur gears, connected to output shaft.

together. The gear trains provide a fixed ratio of propeller shaft speed to engine speed.

In most cases lubrication is with engine oil but in some gear oil is specified. In all cases, only use the oil recommended by the engine or gearbox manufacturer.

General use

Although some gearboxes will survive being put in reverse at full engine speed, it is far safer to reduce engine speed to tickover when changing gear either way. Helical gearboxes will withstand more punishment than metal-to-metal cone clutch types but sympathetic use will extend the life of the clutch, and possibly the skipper as well.

Saildrive units

Saildrives have integral gearboxes and drive the propeller via a bevel gear train and integral propeller shaft, rather like an outboard engine. They need to be lubricated and maintained to manufacturer's recommendations.

Hydraulic drives

These consist of a constant displacement pump driven by the engine which forces hydraulic oil down high pressure tubes to turn a constant displacement motor which drives the propeller shaft.

The ratio of the pump's displacement to the motor gives the drive ratio. A system, for example, with a pump of 50cm³/rev and a motor of 100cm³/rev will give a ratio of 2:1. The propeller speed is therefore 50 per cent of the engine speed.

Hydraulic drives have numerous

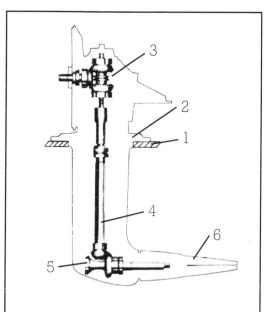

Saildrives resemble an outboard, dispensing with conventional sterngear and emerging from the boat's hull direct. 1 Hull. 2 Seal. 3 Ahead/astern/neutral gears. 4 Drive shaft. 5 Bevel gear. 6 Folding propeller.

advantages over conventional drives. They can, for instance, be reversed at full engine speed without any damage. A control valve limits the system pressure to a safe level.

If the propeller jams the pressure control will again allow the oil to bypass the pump, thus limiting stresses on the propeller shaft and the engine.

The main advantage, however, is that the engine can be practically anywhere in the boat as the connections to the motor are through flexible pipes.

Hydraulic drives are manufactured to industrial standards for continuous duty and therefore have an extremely long life.

The main disadvantage of hydraulic drives is that the system has to have an adequate-sized oil reservoir, which means a heavy one, to obtain reasonable life from the hydraulic oil. The efficiency of the drive is also lower than that of a conventional gearbox and to keep the system running at the optimum temperature a raw water/oil cooler must be fitted.

Maintenance of hydraulic drives

Debris in the oil will reduce the life and efficiency of a hydraulic drive. The pump components are manufactured to extremely small tolerances, measured in microns. Any foreign matter, particularly of a metallic nature, is likely to cause damage. A filter to a minimum standard of ISO BSI/5/15 level 17/11 must be fitted, and the element changed in accordance with a maintenance programme or when the clogging indicator moves into the danger zone.

Water in the oil reservoir will cause the same problems as it does in a fuel tank, and the tank breather must be fitted with a filter.

Finally, low oil level can lead to pump failure. Any air bubbles that get into the system can implode inside the pump when compressed to the working pressure. A level gauge should be fitted.

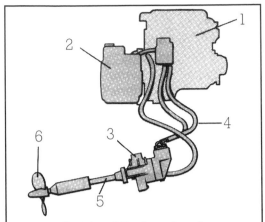

Hydraulic drive. 1 Engine, placed wherever most convenient. 2 Hydraulic pump. 3 Hydraulic motor. 4 Flexible pipes between motor and pump. 5 Propeller shaft. 6 Propeller.

9 Avoiding disasters

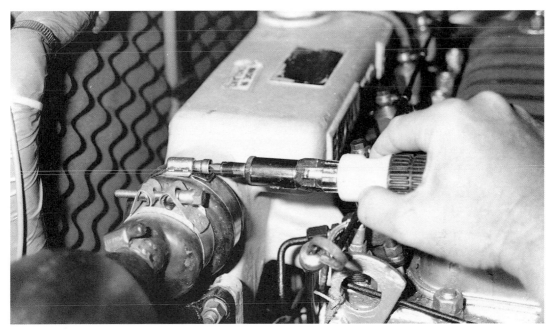

Little things can lead to big disasters. Engines have overheated and yachts have been disabled for the want of a screwdriver to tighten a cooling system hose clip.

It is vital that all skippers establish a pattern of routine engine checks. The first checklist applies when the engine is stopped, the second when it is running. The checks only take a few minutes and should be undertaken every two or three days if you intend to use the engine daily – every week or so if it is used infrequently.

CHECKS WITH THE ENGINE STOPPED

Remove the starter key and switch the batteries off. Then, using an electric torch and a mirror, look for or check:

1. Cooling water leaks (Chapter 4).
2. Stern gland leaks (Chapter 7).
3. Fuel leaks (Chapter 2).
4. Lubricating oil level and condition (Chapter 5).
5. Fresh water coolant level (Chapter 4).
6. Drive belt tension (Chapter 6).
7. Dirt in the pre-filter (Chapter 2).
8. Engine mountings (Chapter 7).
9. Exhaust connections (Chapter 4).
10. Electrical wiring (Chapter 6).

NOTE: Keeping the engine clean will make it much easier to see any leaks or problems.

A leaking water pipe can often be temporarily repaired by wrapping the hole or split first in several layers of tape – ordinary electrical will do – and putting a hose clamp round the 'bodge' as a get-you-home measure. Ideally a spare, correctly-angled hose should be carried, or a length of reinforced hose cut over-long to avoid kinking.

Cooling water leaks

Water leaking from a hose or fitting over the engine can cause extensive long-term damage and soon affect the operation of electrical equipment. Very little electrical equipment fitted to engines is truly waterproof and terminals are especially vulnerable to corrosion and failure. To make matters worse, drive belts tend to pick up the water from any leaks and throw it liberally over the engine compartment.

If you see signs of a leak, first try tightening the fittings. If a hose has failed, replace it. Or, if you don't carry a spare, patch it up as best you can for the time being until a replacement can be obtained.

Always take special care with any fittings sealed with low-friction PTFE tape. They can easily be overtightened, and perhaps cracked. As an alternative use a jointing compound or face seal. It is also difficult to remove PTFE from female threads, and tiny amounts can be scraped off when the fitting is tightened. PTFE debris then circulates in the water system and may block an orifice – often in the thermostat.

The filler cap on fresh water cooling systems should be removed and the water level checked when the engine is cold. It should be just below the neck of the cap. There is invariably some water loss after the header tank is initially filled up as the engine reaches working temperature. After a few checks the normal cold level can be established. If the header tank needs frequent topping up to maintain this level there is a leak in the system, which should be traced and remedied.

Stern gland leaks

A leaky propeller shaft seal or stern gland is fairly normal. A few drops per hour pose no real threat, but the flow always tends to increase and it is better to stop any leaks

The cooling system removes around a third of an engine's heat. The filler cap on this heat exchanger also acts as a pressure valve. Warning lights or a buzzer may well alert you to overheating, but far better to check the water level every day and make sure water is emerging from the exhaust on start up and periodically thereafter.

It is quite normal to find a few drops leaking from a stern gland, but sooner or later the packing will need renewing.

early while you have the chance. Either tighten the gland or force more grease in, but do not overtighten or put too much pressure on the greaser, which can cause wear of the propeller shaft.

Fuel leaks

At best these are messy, at worst they will stop your engine. If the tank is below the engine any fuel leak will result in air being drawn into the system when the engine is stopped. This will make the engine very difficult to start.

Leaks can be from the low pressure side of the system, the drain lines or the high pressure side. Fittings used are normally sealed metal-to-metal or with sealing washers made from aluminium or copper.

Never use jointing compound or PTFE tape to seal fittings in the fuel system. Again, it is virtually impossible to stop tiny particles entering the system and blocking the minute, vital holes and valves in the pumps and injectors.

Fuel leaks need to be dealt with straight away as air or water drawn into the system will stop an engine, especially if the tank is below engine level. This banjo on a fuel return fitting is typical of those found on diesel engines and relies on copper washers for a good seal. Don't use PTFE tape. Before tightening the top bolt check the washers for damage and replace them if necessary. Ideally they should be heated until red to anneal and soften the metal for better bedding down. A clean fuel system like this will be easier to check for leaks.

The flexible shaft of this dipstick makes it easier to reinsert into the hole. The oil level should be between the marks, no higher and certainly no lower.

Lubricating oil

Diesel engines normally use a little more oil than petrol engines and the colour of new oil quickly becomes black. The dipstick indicates the level and condition of the oil. If the level goes up and the oil is discoloured – grey or white, for instance – that's a sure sign it is contaminated with water. This may be due to failure of a gasket or seal in the engine and generally involves a major repair. Running with contaminated oil will result in bearing failures. In an emergency replace the oil, but keep the speed low.

The colour of the oil on the dipstick provides the first clue to an engine's well-being. Grey means water contamination. Oil should be changed in line with the manufacturers instructions.

If a fitting or pipe cannot be sealed by tightening, check for corrosion of the aluminium washers, fatigue cracks in high pressure pipes or cracks in fittings. Replace suspect parts, taking care not to overtighten.

When leaving the boat for a few days or more remove the cover from the engine compartment to allow air to circulate. This will reduce condensation in the compartment as the engine cools, thus reducing the likelihood of corrosion.

If you regularly have to top up to maintain the correct level, refer to Chapter 5. Always keep enough oil on board for a complete oil change.

Oil changes should be made in line with the engine manufacturer's recommendations – normally 100 or 200 hours or at the end of every season, whichever is sooner.

Drive belt tension

Check with your finger to ensure the belt movement is within the manufacturer's recommendations – normally ± 12mm (1/2in). Drive belt slippage can result in slow water pump and alternator speeds, but overtightening will reduce the life of their bearings.

Engine mountings

Check visually and then feel the mountings. Tighten any loose nuts, normally from the bottom, to keep the engine in alignment. Retighten the lock nut on top. If they are found to be very loose the engine may need to be realigned.

Exhaust connections

Check the exhaust visually. If there are any signs of blowing, tighten up the fitting, or repair/replace the hose. Leaking exhaust fumes will quickly fill the boat and cover the engine and its compartment with a sticky black soot.

Electrical wiring

Diesel engines do not need electrical power to run, but most need it to start and some to stop. Most have an alternator or generator to charge the battery, but electrical and battery terminals can vibrate loose, so check them well.

Fan belt tension should be ±12mm (¹/₂in). Drive belt slippage can result in slow water pump and alternator speeds, but over-tightening will reduce bearing life.

The mounting bolts are first loosened, and the alternator body tensioned against the belt, using the shaft of a hammer or similar if necessary.

CHECKS WITH THE ENGINE RUNNING

With the engine running at cruising revs, and taking care not to catch hair, scarf, fingers etc in any moving parts, examine the engine with a torch for water leaks, fuel leaks, oil leaks and excessive vibration.

Water leaks

Water leaks are often easier to trace when the engine is running at operating temperature. On engines with indirect cooling a leak between the freshwater coolant in the sealed system and the raw water from outside – which can, of course, be either fresh or salt – will generally result in water overflowing from the filler cap overflow pipe.

This is caused by raw water contaminating the freshwater system. You'll generally find that the leak is in the heat exchanger or the connections to it and will need to be cured when the engine is stopped. The freshwater system should then be flushed and refilled with the recommended water/antifreeze mixture to stop any corrosion in the water ways.

Fuel leaks

Check the entire fuel system for the smallest trace of leaks. These can only be

This bolt on a sliding stop regulates the alternator position relative to the belt, and hence tension. Two spanners may be needed to undo it.

This alternator is being jammed in place by a bar while the bolts are finally tensioned.

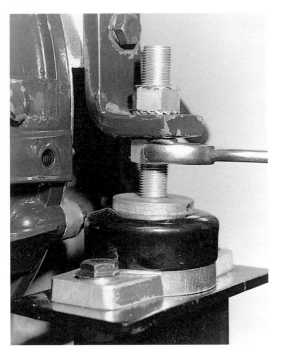 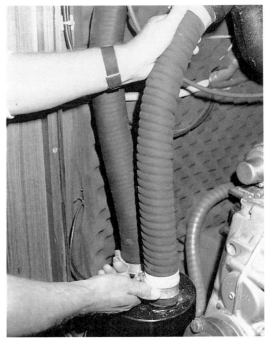

A spanner on the bottom nut of this engine mounting will enable small changes to be made to engine height, but there is no substitute for professional alignment.

All exhaust piping should ideally be double-clipped. Vibration will work loose the tightest clips, allowing water into the boat and/or the engine to overheat.

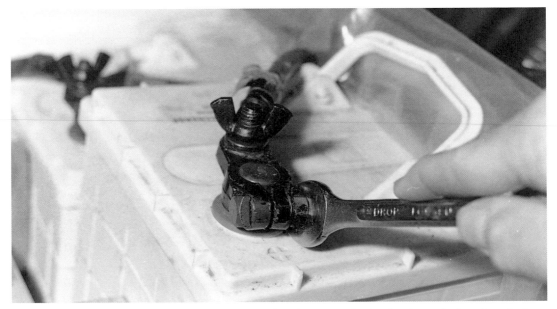

A common cause of the engine failing to respond to the starter button is a loose battery terminal. Grease and periodically tighten the terminals as part of a full electrical and charging circuit check over.

A clean engine makes troubleshooting that much easier. Water or oil leaks are then easily spotted and can be rectified. Flaking paint on an old engine could mean localised overheating.

cured properly with the engine stopped.

Lubricating oil leaks

There are very few engines that have no oil leaks and a couple of drops are no more than a nuisance. If the leak is more serious, however, keep tabs on it, top up the level as required and solve the problem as soon as possible.

When replacing gaskets, plugs or seals always make sure that the area is clean and use the manufacturer's replacement parts. Rubber seals can be manufactured in many types of material, the commonest being

nitrile for mineral oils, neoprene for water.

To avoid pollution, dispose of oily bilge water as you would used lubricating oil – in a proper disposal facility in a marina or garage.

Excessive vibration

This can be caused by a number of factors, including the engine not firing on one cylinder, engine-to-propeller shaft misalignment and loose mountings. Stop the engine before attempting to cure the problem.

Essential tools

Assorted screwdrivers from small
  electrical upwards, flat and
  crosshead
Set of imperial and/or metric
  (depending on engine) combined
  open-ended/ring spanners
  preferably with slim jaws to ease
  access to inaccessible nuts and
  bolts
3/8in and 1/4in drive socket set with
  imperial and metric sockets
Set of imperial and/or metric hexagon
  keys
Right-angled screwdrivers
Feeler gauges

Selection of files
Slipjoint wrench (water pump pliers)
Longnose pliers, standard pliers, wire
  cutters
Any special tools required for engine
Hacksaw and spare blades
Heavy duty knife
Digital multimeter
3in diameter mirror (or larger)
Loctite Lock'n Seal
Soldering iron
Aerosol can of water inhibiting oil
8in adjustable spanner
10in 'Mole' grips
Seizing wire

Service schedule

Read the manufacturer's handbook
and follow the servicing
recommendations. A typical schedule
might be:

Every few days
Basic pre-checks
Pre-filter drain
Check sea water strainer

Every 100 hours
Water separator drain
Pre-filter change
Fine filter change
Oil change
Oil filter change
Gearbox oil check

Annually
Fan belt change
Water pump impeller check
Check hoses and clips
Anode change
Clean or change air filter element
Change gearbox oil

As necessary
Service injectors
Top end overhaul

10 Good engine practice

To start a diesel engine after a long lay-up or a change of lubricating oil filter you will need to follow a few simple steps.

First put the gearbox into neutral. Open the raw water and fuel valves, lift the exhaust valve decompression levers if fitted and hand crank the engine about 20 revs. Alternatively, activate the stop solenoid/stop cable, then turn the engine over 20 or so times on the starter motor. Either way, you are circulating lubricating oil around the engine.

Now start the engine, setting the speed control at 1200-1500rpm, unless the manufacturer's instructions are different. Some engines need full speed, ie maximum fuel.

Initially, use the engine's cold start aids, such as glow plugs, inlet heaters or extra fuel.

After the engine starts, run it at 1200-1500rpm without load for a few minutes to warm up and check that:
1. Water is coming from the exhaust outlet.
2. The green oil pressure light is off.
3. The amber light on the charging circuit is off.

Starting normally

In warm weather most engines will not need any cold start procedure and will fire

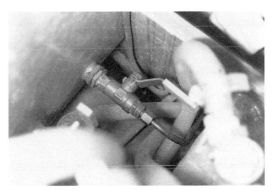

The fuel cut-off valve should be pointed out to all crew members. Handle in-line is on. It should be sited close to the tank but outside the engine compartment in case of fire.

immediately. But slow running engines may need their cold starting aid, especially if it is the type that delivers extra fuel.

With the gearbox in neutral, engine water and fuel valves on, start the engine using

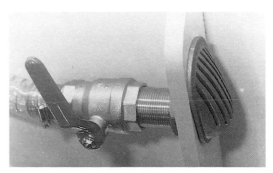

The water inlet strainer is the first line of defence against large debris entering the cooling system. It can easily become clogged with weed or marine growth and crustaceans, restricting water flow, causing overheating.

This two-cylinder engine is fitted with exhaust valve lifters (decompression levers) which make hand-starting feasible. Raise the levers, or in this case push them over to the open position. Crank a few times to prime fuel and get the flywheel moving.

When the engine is turning over as fast as you can crank it, drop the levers. This will close the exhaust valves and give the engine the compression it needs to fire.

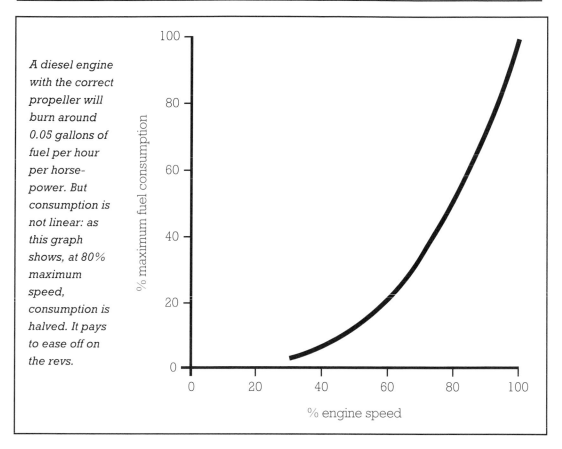

A diesel engine with the correct propeller will burn around 0.05 gallons of fuel per hour per horse-power. But consumption is not linear: as this graph shows, at 80% maximum speed, consumption is halved. It pays to ease off on the revs.

% maximum fuel consumption

% engine speed

the starter motor, by pushing the button or turning the key. If the engine is reluctant to start, go back to the cold starting procedure. Reluctance to start can be due to sticky injectors. They will need servicing.

Older engines fitted with combined starter/generators, or a hand crank, will need to have their exhaust valve decompression levers lifted before the engine will turn. Once the flywheel is turning at speed, the levers are dropped, the exhaust valves close and the engine should start.

If the engine doesn't start within 20 seconds or so, switch off the key, wait for all moving parts to stop and try again after a pause to

The energy in a boat's wash comes from the engine, so high powered semi-displacement craft such as this one burn a lot of fuel.

let the starter motor cool. If it still won't start, turn off the raw cooling water at the inlet valve to prevent the exhaust filling

This solenoid-operated stop switch will give little trouble, but malfunction is unlikely to be easy to fix. A good troubleshooter will be able to pinpoint the problem and rig a manual stop cable.

The speed of a displacement boat is limited by its waterline length. Even a high-powered engine will not be able to push a boat with a waterline length of 25ft beyond about 6.5 knots.

with water which could then flow back through the exhaust valves into the engine.

When it does start, remember to turn the water back on and check that:
1. Water is coming from the exhaust.
2. The green oil pressure light is off or the gauge is registering.
3. The amber light in the charging circuit is off or the voltmeter is registering 13+ volts.

Turbocharged engines should be run for a few minutes at low speed to warm up before any load is applied, or according to the manufacturer's instructions.

Using the engine

A boat's optimum cruising speed naturally depends on its design, displacement or weight, propeller size and the power of its engine. The speed of a displacement, as opposed to planing, hull is subject to a mathematical formula based on its waterline length (see below).

Pushing any displacement boat even a little bit faster than its design speed will require disproportionately more power, although alowance must be made for strong winds and head seas.

Similarly an inland waterways boat needs enough power to overcome currents and strong winds.

With the maximum speed established it is generally better to cruise at 20 per cent below the maximum under normal conditions as this will work the engine reasonably hard, give an acceptable boat speed and low fuel consumption – as low as half the top-speed consumption.

Speed formula

The maximum theoretical speed of a displacement hull is approximately 1.3 x square root of its waterline length in feet. A yacht with a waterline length of 36ft would, therefore, be capable of 1.3 x 6, or approximately 8 knots. Remember that boat speed on inland waterways may also be limited by waterway regulations.

Engine manufacturers produce graphs showing what size engine will drive any given boat at its designed speed, and what propeller should be fitted. Output torque is roughly proportional to the engine's cubic capacity and output power is proportional to torque and speed.

Routine use

Most engines need warming up. Running them for 10 minutes or so will also charge the batteries. Then you can start your routine checks:
1. Oil pressure: check that the oil pressure light is off, the buzzer is silent or the gauge is reading the recommended pressure.
2. Check the cooling water temperature gauge: if it is higher than usual check the cooling water supply to the engine. See Chapter 4 for possible causes.
3. Listen to the noise of the engine running. If you hear anything unusual reduce engine speed, put the gearbox in neutral and investigate. Debris around the propeller is a prime suspect especially if the noise stops when neutral is selected.

If you're running the engine continuously, make a visual engine check with the aid of a torch every 7-10 hours, taking care to keep clear of all moving parts.

Shutting down the engine

Reduce engine speed to tick-over, select neutral on the gearbox, and press the fuel stop switch or pull the stop cable. Do not turn off the key switch before the engine has stopped as, in some cases, it can damage the electrical system.

The stop cable or stop switch operates a cut-off valve on the fuel injection pump. When the engine is stopped reset the stop mechanism (if a cable is used) and only then turn the starter key to the off position.

Turbocharged engines may need to be run at low speed off load for a while before stopping. Refer to the engine manufacturer's instructions.

Sailing with engine stopped

After the engine is stopped engage reverse gear to lock the shaft and prevent the propeller rotating in the boat's wake, or wear can occur in the gearbox and the stern gland.

On yachts with folding propellers put the control lever into the fold position. On yachts with two-bladed propellers line up the propeller with the keel to reduce drag. Mark the inner end of the propeller shaft or coupling to indicate the propeller position from inside the boat.

Inland waterways

Boats with inboard engines used on canals and rivers are normally heavy and the key requirement is high output torque to provide sufficient power to drive as large a propeller as possible. This requirement, although useful on a yacht or seagoing motorboat, is not essential and there is a tendency therefore for two lines of development: low speed, high torque engines for inland waterway craft, and higher speed, lighter weight engines for seagoing craft.

11 Troubleshooting Flow Chart

Problem	Possible Causes
Starter motor will not turn when switched on Refer to chapter 6	If lights are dim, battery is discharged
	If lights are bright, starter wiring could be loose or disconnected
	Battery connections loose or wiring corroded
	Starter switch loose or disconnected
	Jammed starter motor
Starter motor tries to turn engine but engine will not turn Refer to chapter 6	If lights are dim, battery voltage is reduced
	Water in engine
	Loose or corroded wiring
Starter motor turns engine but engine will not start Refer to chapter 2	Air in fuel
	Fuel isolator valve closed
	Insufficient fuel in tank
	Engine stop valve closed
	Engine speed control cable disconnected
	Clogged pre filter/water separator
	Clogged fine filter
	Lift pump not working
Engine overheating Refer to chapter 4	Raw water intake obstructed
	Pump impeller broken
	Thermostat blocked or defective
	Engine water passages blocked
Black smoke from exhaust Refer to chapters 3, 7	Propeller fouled
	Exhaust restricted
	Engine starved of air
Propeller will not turn with engine running Refer to chapter 8	Propeller fallen off or drive key sheared
	Flexible coupling displaced or drive key sheared
	Forward/reverse cable disconnected from gearbox
Excessive vibration/noise Refer to chapters 5,7	Propeller fouled
	Engine mounting loose or broken
	Drive shaft coupling loose
	Loss of lubricating oil or pressure

Remedial Action

Notes

Switch to alternative battery or possibly handstart. Try starting with decompression lever engaged	Check charging system Alternatively, battery may be dead
Check wiring and correct	
Tighten	
Check and correct	
Release or remove and release	Ascertain reason for jamming

Switch to alternative battery or possibly handstart. Try starting with decompression lever engaged	Check charging system
Turn water inlet valve off. Remove injectors and turn engine over and remove as much water as possible from cylinder head. Change lubricating oil, which will have been contaminated by the water in the engine.	Turn water on again after starting
Check wiring and correct	

Bleed fuel system	Most common reason for engine not starting
Open isolator valve	Leave the valve open at all times unless there is a specific need to close it
Put in fuel	Bleed fuel system
Release cable or solenoid	Correct reason for it sticking
Reconnect	
Remove, clean, fit new filter. Bleed system	
Change element. Bleed system	Keep at least one spare element on board
Repair or replace	Keep spare on board

Clear intake	
Turn inlet water off. Replace impeller	Turn water on again before starting
Turn inlet water off and remove	
	Major strip down required

Remove fouling	Try reversing propeller several times at low speed to release
Check exhaust run from engine through lockers	
Remove obstruction	

Sail to safe haven!	
Rectify if possible	
Reconnect	

Remove fouling	Try reversing propeller several times at low speed to release
Tighten nuts/bolts. Replace broken parts	
Reconnect	
Investigate, refill	Engine bearings may be damaged

12 Troubleshooting in more detail

The starter motor makes no attempt to turn

1. Check that the battery connections are tight, clean and greased. The starter motor needs a high current, so it is essential that there is no resistance due to corrosion or looseness at the battery connections or in the wiring.

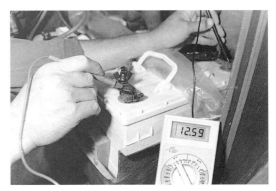

If the terminals are tight, a voltmeter across them will show immediately if the battery is producing the correct voltage, in the case of a 12-volt battery anything up to 14 volts.

The first port of call in any problem involving a failure of the starter motor to turn the engine is the battery. Check the terminals.

2. Check that the connections to the starter motor and battery selector switch are tight and clean for the same reasons as in 1.

3. Check the battery voltage, especially if the motor is trying to turn the engine but failing to do so. Use a voltmeter or multimeter. Alternatively, switch a cabin light on to give a rough idea of battery state.

4. Check the switch wiring. Starter switches often use push-on terminals. Check these for looseness or corrosion.

5. The starter motor may be jammed. Rotate the engine by hand to free, and try again.

The starter motor turns the engine but it will not start

1. Check that there is fuel in the tank and the isolator valve is open.

2. Check that the engine stop valve is open. Cable-operated valves are easy to leave in the off position. Electrically-operated valves can jam in the closed position, or the return spring may become disconnected or break.

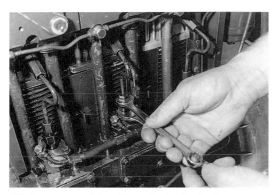 

High pressure bleeding. Air in the fuel system needs to be 'chased' through methodically, starting from the low pressure (tank) side before moving on to the high pressure (injector) side. If the system is clear up to the fine fuel filter, bleed forward, undoing the pump bleed screws, while continuing to pump fuel through by hand. Start with the injector nearest the pump.

If the problem is on the low pressure side, vent the fine filter by undoing the nut, usually on the side (see manual) a few turns only, all the while pumping the fuel through using the thumb cam on the fuel pump body. Once pure fuel is bleeding, retighten the nut against the pressure of your thumb.

3. Check that the fuel lift pump is working by operating it manually and that there is fuel flowing from the vent screw in the low pressure system. This is usually on the filter.

4. Check that the engine speed control – throttle – is connected and working correctly.

5. Check the high pressure piping from the high pressure pump to the injectors for leaks. Pipes can fail, fatigue cracks can develop and union nuts may work loose.

6. Check that the fuel pre-filter is not clogged, by inspection. If no pre-filter is fitted (only a water separator) then

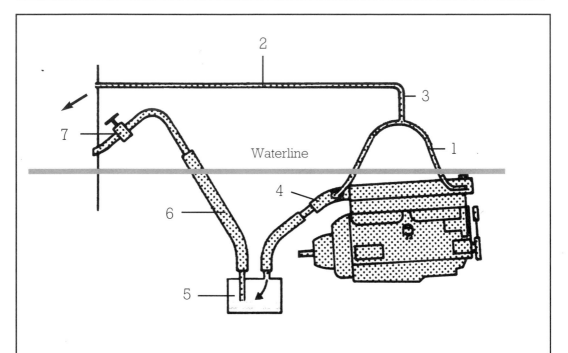

An overheating exhaust can melt the water trap, burn the hoses and cause a fire. A waterlock system at its simplest comprises: 1 Cooling water pipe looped above waterline. 2 Small bore pipe for bleed overboard, or a vacuum relief valve can be fitted at 3. 4 Water injection bend. 5 Waterlock/silencer chamber. 6 Outlet pipe. 7 Exhaust shut-off valve.

check the fine filter is not clogged by opening the bleed screws and manually operating the lift pump.

7. Check all low pressure fuel piping for leaks, especially if the tank is situated below or level with the engine.

8. The most likely cause is air in the fuel system. Bleed the fuel system of air as described in Chapter 2. (A leak in the low pressure part of the system will not necessarily be evident, as it will suck in air rather than expel fuel.) Check all connections on the low pressure side of the fuel system for tightness.

The starter motor tries to turn the engine without success

1. The most likely cause is reduced battery voltage, so check voltage as described above. Engines which depend on an electric starter motor should have their own, dedicated battery.

2. Water in the engine will also stop the engine turning. Water entering via the exhaust pipe – large following seas can force water back up the exhaust – or via the head gasket can stop the pistons moving. Trying to start the engine with water in the cylinder(s) can break the crankshaft, pistons or connecting rods.

Exhaust water traps, goose necks, check valves and anti-syphon devices can all reduce the chances of this occurring. If water is suspected, remove the injectors and try turning the engine over.

The engine is overheating

The common symptoms of an overheated engine are:

1. Engine noise changes. It may sound laboured.

2. The temperature gauge shows an increase over normal.

3. Smoke. This can be caused by a burning exhaust and/or, if the exhaust is water cooled, the plastic water trap melting.

4. No water coming out of the exhaust or water outlet.

5. The engine stops, or seizes completely.

Cooling water flow to the engine can be interrupted for a number of reasons:

1. An obstruction such as plastic bag blocking the water intake. This can be difficult to pinpoint, but when the engine is stopped the obstruction may float free. A water inlet filter with a clear top will enable the incoming water supply to be monitored.

2. The intake valve may be closed or obstructed. Debris such as barnacles and weed can gather in the valve. Valves need to be checked and cleaned when laid up. Once again, an inlet filter with a clear top will help.

Easy access to all parts of the engine will make routine maintenance easier and emergencies less traumatic. This engine installation aboard the author's boat is some years old.

3. Accumulation of salt deposits and debris in the engine waterways. These can build up and stop the water circulating effectively. This is always a problem in raw-water-cooled engines. Good laying up procedures (see Chapter 13) can extend the period between major cooling system overhauls. The effectiveness of a heat exchanger in indirect systems can also be reduced by salt and debris.

If the engine is overheating, check that the cooling water intake valve is open (handle in line with pipe).

The best tool to remove an impeller is a slipjoint wrench. Impellers come in many sizes, some with shaft locking spindles that must be unscrewed before the impeller can be freed. On reassembly make sure the pump body faces are clean, fit the blades with the correct 'set', fit a new gasket and grease the impeller.

4. The pump impeller may be damaged or broken. Most pumps use a rubber vane-type impeller. These have a hard life and eventually the vanes may break off. Impellers are normally easy to change but you must always retrieve any rubber debris and broken vanes from the system to avoid blocking the waterways.

The impeller may also fail if the bond between the metal centre and the rubber fails. The impeller is one of the first casualties of an engine that is starved of water. Since it depends on water for lubrication, if the pump has run dry check the impeller. If it is damaged replace it, making sure to give the vanes the correct initial set, according to the direction of rotation. A dab of light grease or petroleum jelly will help.

5. Failure of the thermostat. If the thermostat fails closed it will prevent cooling water circulating properly around the engine, and overheating can result. If you suspect the thermostat, remove it temporarily. The engine will run cooler, and therefore less efficiently, but should not suffer any damage if run for a short period.

The engine produces black smoke

This is caused by the engine being overloaded – being asked to produce more power than it is capable of – because:

1. The propeller has been fouled by a rope or other debris, fishing nets etc.

2. The propeller is too large for the engine.

The thermostat lies under a housing, usually easily accessible at the front of the engine. Overheating can be caused by the valve sticking, but too great a flow in cold weather will prevent the engine reaching optimum temperature.

Unscrew thermostat housing, remove thermostat and clean seating and surrounding waterways.

The correct opening can be tested by immersing in water at the temperature stamped on the thermostat body, usually 74°C. If in doubt replace, as thermostats are not repairable.

Gear levers and bowden cables can become stiff with time. Before using brute force, check that nothing has jammed the cable and make sure the gearbox itself is not jammed by working the lever on the housing.

3. The exhaust is restricted, perhaps flattened by equipment as it passes through a stern locker, for example.

4. The injection timing is incorrect. Check that the bolts holding the high pressure pump to the engine are tight.

5. The engine is starved of air. Check that the engine compartment vents are not obstructed and the inlet filter on the engine is clean.

The engine runs but the propeller will not turn

This is often due to there simply being no connection between engine and propeller for one of a variety of reasons:

1. The propeller has fallen off.

2. The drive key in the flexible coupling has fallen out or has sheared, or the drive key in the propeller has been displaced/sheared. The first can be checked visually, and replaced. The second at best will require a diver, at worst a haul-out.

3. The gearbox has seized. Little can be done without professional help.

4. The forward/reverse cable/link has become disconnected from the

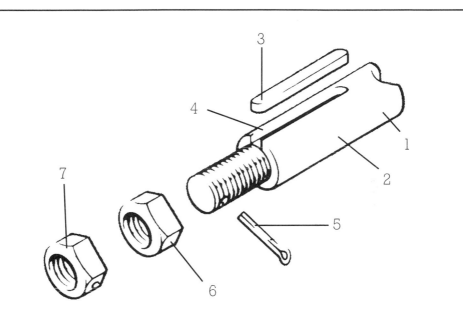

Propeller/shaft connection. 1 Shaft. 2 Tapered portion. 3 Key. 4 Keyway. 5 Split pin for lock nut. 6 Propeller nut. 7 Lock nut.

gearbox. Reconnect or operate the selection lever directly at the gearbox. This can cause manoeuvring problems in marinas and close to other boats!

The engine stops occasionally

This can be caused by overheating or reduction of air flow to the engine. Engines need substantial amounts of air to operate correctly and starvation causes the engine to run erratically or stop. There are two possible causes:

1. The engine air inlet filter may be blocked.

2. The inlet vents to the engine compartment may be obstructed either by people or equipment such as liferafts, lifebuoys, ropes, etc. A

blocked tank vent can also stop fuel flowing into the engine fuel system.

The engine produces blue or white smoke

This is generally associated with a worn engine. The engine is burning lubricating oil, which is entering the combustion chambers because of:

1. Worn pistons/rings.

2. Worn valve guides.

3. A leaking head gasket.

The battery is not being charged when the engine is running

Although diesel engines do not require electricity to run, they do need to produce

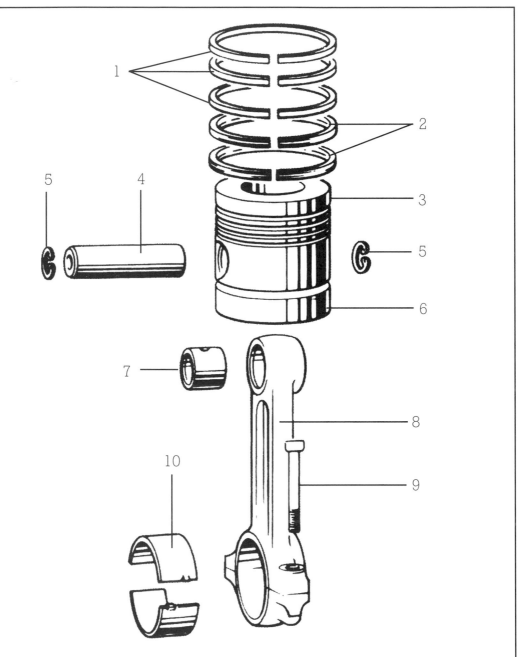

The piston and connecting rod are usually the first major components to become damaged if the engine overheats. Worn cylinders and broken rings can cause low compression, reluctance to start and excessive oil consumption. Big end wear can be caused by low oil pressure. 1 Compression rings. 2 Oil control rings. 3 Piston. 4 Gudgeon pin. 5 Circlips. 6 Piston skirt. 7 Small end bearing. 8 Connecting rod. 9 Bolt. 10 Big end bearing.

electricity if the battery is to be recharged and the demands from the boat's electrical system met. The most likely causes of not charging are:

1. The drive belt to the alternator is loose or slipping. This can be tightened relatively easily.

2. Wiring from the alternator to the electrical system is loose or corroded. Check all connections. NOTE: electrical disconnection of the alternator from the battery while it is running will burn out the diodes built into the alternator to convert the AC output of the alternator to direct current.

The battery is being overcharged

The output from an alternator is self-regulating, but sometimes a separate sensing wire is used. If this is broken or disconnected the alternator will produce its maximum output, regardless. This will overcharge the battery and cause gassing and boiling over, resulting in spillage of acid and battery failure. The gas produced is also inflammable. If the ammeter shows abnormally high charge rates, check the sensing wiring.

Engine revs apparently drop

The tachometer, or engine speed meter, often runs off an electrical output signal from the alternator, which is driven by a belt. So, if the engine appears to be running normally yet the rev counter indicates otherwise, the first thing to check is whether the drive belt is slipping. In many cases the belt also drives the raw water pump, so the engine will also suffer from reduced water flow and may overheat.

Excess vibration or noise

Diesel engines tend to be noisy but flexible mounts and reasonable acoustic insulation reduce this to an acceptable level. If unusual noise or vibration is experienced there are several possible causes:

1. A rope or other debris around the propeller hitting the hull as the prop rotates. This will cause the propeller to spin out of balance and vibrate.

2. A loose P or A bracket.

3. A loose or broken engine mounting.

4. Drive coupling to propeller shaft loose.

5. Engine oil lost or water in the oil causing engine damage.

A loose engine mounting can cause severe propeller shaft vibration and excessive strain on the P or A bracket and/or the stern gland. Water could then leak into the boat, at worst causing it to sink.

Diesel engine problems

Symptoms   Possible Causes (see key below)

Symptoms	Possible Causes (see key below)
Engine runs intermittently (starts and stops)	1,2,3,4,5,6,7
Rough idling	1,2,3,4,7,8,9,10,11
Misfiring	2,3,7,8,10,11,13,14,15,16,17,18,19,20,31
Knocking	2,7,8,9,10,11,13,15,18,19,21,22,31
Engine not developing full power	2,3,4,6,7,8,10,13,14,15,16,17,18,19,20,23,24,27,29
Black exhaust smoke	6,7,8,10,14,15,16,17,19,20,23,24,25,27,31
White exhaust smoke	2,10,12,15,16,17,29,31
Blue exhaust smoke	13,23,28,30

Possible causes

1. Idling adjustment too low
2. Air in fuel system
3. Fuel filter choked
4. Fuel lift pump defective
5. Fuel tank nearly empty
6. Dirty air cleaner
7. Sticking valves or rocker arms
8. Dirty or faulty injectors
9. Broken valve spring(s)
10. Wrong injection pump timing
11. Injector pipe(s) loose or defective
12. Water in fuel
13. Defective or sticking piston rings/worn cylinder bores
14. Faulty fuel injection pump
15. Incorrect valve timing
16. Poor compression
17. Leaking cylinder head gasket
18. Engine overheating
19. Incorrect valve (tappet) clearances
20. Defective valve or seats
21. Low oil pressure
22. Defective oil bearings
23. Worn valve guides
24. Dirty or damaged turbocharger
25. Engine overloaded (e.g. wrong propeller or dirty hull bottom)
26. Defective boost control
27. Exhaust pipe restriction
28. Crankcase overfilled
29. Engine overcooled
30. Leaking turbocharger oil sealer
31. Faulty cold start equipment

With thanks to Perkins Engines

13 Laying up

"And then I remembered I hadn't drained the engine"

When a boat is laid up or taken out of commission for a while, a small amount of preparation will pay dividends in extending the life of the engine.

The main enemies are corrosion and frost, and all systems need to be attended to, following the engine manufacturer's recommendations closely as significant differences occur between different makes.

Cooling system

Check hoses, fittings and hose clips for leaks, deterioration and rust. Replace if necessary.

Indirect systems

Drain and flush with clean water, then refill with a mixture of clean water (preferably de-ionised) and antifreeze incorporating a corrosion inhibitor. While flushing the

While the boat is laid up for the winter, take advantage of the opportunity to enrol for a diesel maintenance course, ideally one specific to your engine type. A thorough knowledge of your engine gained in the clinical environment of a workshop or test bench will save you having to identify vital service points for the first time in the cramped, dark confines of an engineroom. But just as important, it should help remind you what that oily lump in the bottom of the boat should look like, and prompt you to apply a little TLC before it becomes neglected ballast, understandably reluctant to start when most needed.

engine, also drain the heat exchanger. Then run the engine until it reaches working temperature to ensure adequate circulation.

If the engine has been running hot, you should remove and clean the heat exchanger. Even if the engine is running at normal temperature it is good practice to clean the tubes occasionally.

All raw water systems

These should be flushed with fresh water by running the engine with the inlet pipe drawing the water from a bucket. Keep the bucket filled until at least 20 litres have been flushed through. Mix the correct amount of antifreeze for the temperatures expected with water in a bucket. Then let the engine draw the mixture into the cooling system until the bucket is empty.

Stop the engine. Alternatives to antifreeze include soluble oil and water, or a mixture of antifreeze, soluble oil and water, both of which inhibit corrosion. Remove the raw water pump impeller.

If the engine has been running hot locally – the paint will be discoloured – you may need to remove the cylinder heads to clean out the engine water passages.

Clean the raw water inlet strainer and inspect the sacrificial anodes fitted to the engine, changing them for new if they are over 50 per cent wasted.

Lubricating system

Change the lubricating oil filter element and pump out the lubricating oil from the sump, or drain through the drainplug and replace with fresh oil. If the boat is to be laid up for a long period use an inhibiting oil, but this must be replaced when the engine is recommissioned. See Chapter 5 for oil specifications.

Air system

Clean the air intake strainer or inspect the paper element. These are often dirty in one area only, and can be turned round to extend their life. If in doubt replace, as a restriction in the air intake will cause combustion problems – remember, an engine needs far more air than it does fuel. Finally, tape over the inlet to stop air circulating inside the combustion chambers.

Fuel system

Fill up to keep the air in the tank to a minimum, thereby minimising condensation. Every five years you should pump out the bottom layer of fuel, water and debris into a suitable container and dispose of it responsibly.

If the arrangement allows it, a sump at the bottom of the fuel tank, which can be drained through a cock, will allow you to always keep the fuel tank clean. This is worth considering if you have to install new tanks for any reason.

Finally, check externally for rust and leaks, especially around the bottom of the tank if it is made from metal.

Engine

Check all piping for leaks and rectify any problems. The injectors should then be removed, and a few squirts of upper cylinder or lay-up lubricant directed into the injector pockets. If possible slowly turn the engine one revolution by hand to distribute the lubricant. Do not use the starter motor in case there is too much lubricant in the cylinder, which would damage the engine. If the engine has been reluctant to start, have the injectors serviced before refitting them. Replace sealing washers when refitting the injectors.

General maintenance

Clean the engine and check the mountings to ensure that the nuts and bolts are tight. If there has been any problem previously with an engine mounting becoming loose, check the alignment of the propeller shaft. Check also the mounting brackets for cracks.

Loosen the alternator and water pump drive belt and remove it. Check for wear and replace.

Plug the exhaust exit to avoid air blowing through the engine. Some of the exhaust valves in multi-cylinder engines will be open when the engine is stopped. Finally, spray all exposed metal parts except the alternator with water-inhibiting oil.

Batteries

Remove the batteries, check their condition, top them up with distilled water if necessary and charge. Batteries should be stored in a dry place and charged once a month.

Outdrives and saildrives

These should be drained and the lubricating oil replaced. Sacrificial anodes should also be checked and replaced if below 50 per cent of their original mass. Finally, check all bellows, seals and hoses and replace any that appear damaged in any way.

14 Onboard engine spares

Inevitably, even on the best installed and serviced engines, things will go wrong, pipe clips will break and impellers will become damaged. Every boat should carry a minimum of spares to solve most common problems.

Spares (minimum requirements)

2 water pump impellers and gaskets
1 oil filter element
1 pre-filter element
1 fine fuel filter element
Sufficient lubricating oil to refill engine
Selection of electrical wiring terminations
Engine operator's handbook and list of agents
Gearbox operator's handbook
Fuel lift pump repair kit or complete pump
Drive belt fan for water pump/alternator
Roll of self-amalgamating repair tape
Selection of hose clamps
Petroleum jelly

Spares for extended cruising

2 water pump impellers
1 water pump repair kit
2 or more fine fuel filter cratridges
2 or more air filter cartridges

Sufficient lubricating oil to refill twice
Selection of electrical terminations & wiring
Stern gland packing material
Engine operator's handbook and workshop manual and list of agents
Gearbox operator's handbook and workshop manual and list of agents
Fuel lift pump and repair kit
Spare set of injectors
Joint and gasket kit
Spare anodes if fitted
Set of water hoses
A quantity of de-ionised water } For topping up
A quantity of antifreeze } freshwater system
External return springs for high pressure fuel pump (if fitted)
2 sets aluminium or copper washers for high pressure fuel system
2 drive belts for water pump/alternator
1 drive belt for high pressure fuel pump/valve gear if fitted
1 thermostat and gasket for housing
1 freshwater pump repair kit
Selection of hose clamps
Roll of self-amalgamating repair tape
Petroleum jelly
Waterproof grease

THE ENGINE FOR THOSE WHO'D RATHER BE SAILING.

The perfect engine for a sailboat might seem like a contradiction in terms.

But that's just what Lister Marine set out to achieve when we designed the Alpha 20, 30, 40 and the new 55 TURBO marine diesels.

Their modern computer-aided design is compact and lightweight, for neat installation and ease of access down below.

Their combustion technology makes them quiet and low on vibration and emissions, for relaxed motor-sailing.

Their reliability and power will get you out of a tight spot fast, yet is easily controllable when you come to berth in the busiest marina.

Last but not least, their low-maintenance design, long service intervals and the back-up of our worldwide network of Marine Diesel Centres mean you shouldn't spend an hour longer ashore than you have to.

With a Lister Marine Alpha on board life is just what it should be.

Plain sailing.

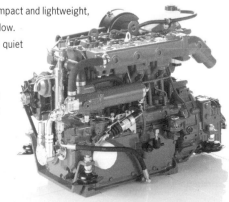

ALPHA
20 • 30 • 40 • 55 TURBO

Lister

MARINE DIESELS

information and the location of Lister Marine Diesel Centres contact Lister-Petter Ltd, Dursley, Gloucestershire GL11 4HS. Tel: (01453) 544141. Fax: (01453) 546732. A member of the BTR Group.

Some relevant titles from Fernhurst Books

If you would like a free full-colour brochure please write, phone or fax us:

**Fernhurst Books,
Duke's Path, High Street, Arundel, West Sussex BN18 9AJ, England**

Telephone: 01903 882277 Fax: 01903 882715